THE TRIAL OF CHAKA DLAMINI

An Economic Scenario for the New South Africa

THE TRIAL OF CHAKA DLAMINI

An Economic Scenario for the New South Africa

STEPHEN MEINTJES & MICHAEL JACQUES

Foreword by THAMI MAZWAI

AMAGI BOOKS

About The Authors:

Stephen Meintjes, 50, is a graduate of Stellenbosch (B. Comm Law) and Oxford (B.A. Juris) and managing director of the investment management operation of a life assurance group based in Johannesburg.

Michael Jacques, 53, is a Chartered Accountant, and a director of a personnel and business consultancy in Sandton.

Amagi Books
P O Box 92385, Norwood 2117
Telephone (011) 442-8898

First Published August 1990

Cover illustration by Chris Page

ISBN No 0-9583105-1-3

Typeset by GraphicSet
Printed and bound by
The Natal Witness Printing & Publishing Company (Pty) Ltd

CONTENTS

Foreword
Introduction
Acknowledgements

1   **Chaka's Trial**   1
        Impatient township youths demand that Chaka explain how
        replacing taxation with a user charge on natural resources can
        help the cause of freedom, justice and prosperity.

2   **Free Land**   8
        Continuing the discussion, Chaka explains how abolishing taxes
        allows labour and capital to keep the full fruit of their
        endeavours. The user charge frees land for full development and
        easy access without confiscation.

3   **The Mad Taxer's Tea Party**   15
        At a lunch party in the northern suburbs, Chaka and some
        friends discuss the complexity of, and damage done by, today's
        taxes.

4   **The Next Great Trek — From Taxes to Rent**   23
        Chaka and his friends present some proposals as to how the
        present tax system could be changed to user charges on natural
        resources.

5   **The Utility Maximisation of Pigeons**   32
        Chaka explains to a sceptical Dr Phalane how the study of
        economics has strayed from the study of Man in Society to
        abstruse mathematical models with little relevance to the real
        world.

6   **Simple is Beautiful**   42
        At Soweto Suzy's shebeen, Chaka and his young friends discuss
        how endless complications arise when the simplicity of rent and
        other basic principles are ignored.

7   **The Thundering Bankherd**   54
        Chaka and Wilson Radebe, a banker, discuss the function of
        banking and how, in a society which imposed a user charge on
        natural resources, it would operate to ease access to credit as well
        as natural resources.

8   **The Boerocrats**   63
      Chaka and his friends meet with some Boers to talk about the
      true role of the Afrikaner in a free South Africa.

9   **Free Men**   68
      On another occasion, the same group discusses freedom, a Bill of
      Rights, the Freedom Charter, political freedom in other
      countries, and how political freedom can be attained in South
      Africa.

10   **Who Owns the Land and How**   81
      At the same gathering, the group discusses systems of land tenure
      in South Africa, both past and present.

11   **Why 'Turbulent' Tutu?**   90
      Chaka explains to a concerned priest why it is the duty of
      religious leaders to speak out against injustice. He uses an
      analogy of expropriating and relocating St. Mary's Cathedral to
      show how user charges can end monopoly and bring about a
      truly free market in the most important market of all — natural
      resources.

12   **Call to the West**   95
      Dr Phalane asks Chaka how the system he proposes for South
      Africa could benefit the so-called capitalist countries of the
      Western world...

13   **Call to the East**   103
      ...and also the countries of the East, and Eastern Europe as they
      start to dismantle their socialist economies.

14   **Broad Sunlit Uplands**   110
      Chaka closes with his vision of a South Africa free, not only from
      apartheid, but also from the yoke of outdated and outlandish
      ideas. The verdict.

Chapter Notes   112

Bibliography   114

FOREWORD

by Thami Mazwai, Editor, Sowetan Business

The land question and the redistribution of wealth will be the major issues on the negotiation table. In fact, as far as most black South Africans are concerned, the liberation struggle centres around the land question.

To whom does it belong?

Also, with the population of the homeless now estimated at more than 7 million, the debate over land will occupy more of our time. Answers must be found, and quickly too.

This book is thus welcome as it expands the search for options as our country agonisingly tries to get on course to create a new society.

Many maintain that the land historically belongs to the indigenous Africans, others say it belongs to all who live in it, while others say it should be owned by those tilling it.

These schools of thought are the basis for the acrimonious, and often deadly, debate among the people of this country.

Stephen Meintjes and Michael Jacques have taken a deeper look at the land crisis and were rocked by what they saw. Their view on what could be a possible solution is summed up in this book.

Their concept might not be all that new; after all the debate on land usage and rent, the concepts of productive and marginal land, have been with us since the days of the feudal system, later including the theories of the classical economists.

What these two South Africans have come up with is a fresher look which takes into account today's dynamics.

Between these covers are ideas which may not be popular with various individuals and political organisations in the country. This is what makes the book a good read, for it does not play up to any political school of thought.

In our fluid and unpredictable situation in which the regular debate and solutions that have until now been tried have fallen far short of meeting the expectations of various communities, it is now time for other ideas.

When President de Klerk unbanned the ANC, PAC and South African Communist Party on February 2, he unleashed a new form of political activity in this country, debate without restrictions.

With this in mind, and the fact that it is our responsibility to forge a new society for our children, let the ideas in this book be looked at with an open mind. They could be slotted into traditional beliefs, accepted in part, or even scrapped in their entirety.

But they must be debated, for only in this manner can solutions to the crisis be found.

INTRODUCTION

This book has been written to facilitate a peaceful settlement in South Africa and to help keep the peace afterwards. It is intended to bridge what otherwise will probably be a fatal gap between the various protagonists in the present political scene in South Africa.

To understand the underlying barrier to peace in South Africa let us look at the requirements of the major players.

— the *ruling minority* wants to retain an effective share in government via some kind of consensus format or minority veto;
— the *authentic black leadership*, on the other hand, is looking to majority rule in a non-racial, democratic state;
— *foreign capital* requires not only the assent of authentic black leadership and the ensuing lifting of sanctions, but an environment conducive to investment; i.e. guarantees against expropriation, excessive taxation and regulation, as well as full repatriation of dividends.

If black leaders are to accept anything less than the full fruits of power and immediate re-distribution of wealth via high taxation and state spending, they will require a very clear-cut quid pro quo that will speedily vindicate their moderation by an increase in prosperity and opportunity for their followers. The adherents of capitalism will argue that this will be achieved by the lifting of sanctions, followed by the inflow of foreign capital and the revival of the capitalist system.

However, the marked failure of communism should not blind us to the fact that all is far from well in the capitalist West. The large underclasses in the United States and endemic unemployment in Western Europe bear eloquent testimony to this.

If prosperity for some amidst poverty and unemployment is the best that capitalism can offer us after apartheid goes, we can well understand the scepticism of black leadership, because, in the South African context, those unemployed and disadvantaged will continue overwhelmingly to be black.

So what is the quid pro quo that black leaders may find acceptable?

The alternative is simply to go the route the West would probably have gone but for the rise of socialism. It was mapped out in the late nineteenth century by the American Henry George in his book *Progress and Poverty* and eagerly propounded by followers such as Winston Churchill and the British Liberal Party in 1910 as well as Tolstoy, Sun Yat-Sen and others.

This approach recognises the prime cause of poverty as being the failure of the community to collect its revenue from its natural source, rent. Rent may be defined as the difference between what may be produced on the least productive site in use and all other land, given the equal application of labour and capital.

Taxation penalises all those who work and risk capital in the creation of wealth. Instead of taxing the product of labour and capital, the community needs to recognise that all who produce benefit to a greater or lesser extent from the land on which they work. By charging them accordingly, it would not only eliminate the disincentive of taxation, but it would provide an unbeatable incentive to work and risk capital.

For whereas taxation penalises the successful producer and protects the inefficient, a user charge on land allows the successful to reap the full fruits of their labour and capital. A user charge on land would also penalise the idle hoarder and weed out the inefficient. By simply charging the producer for that which he receives from the community, namely, the value of the site on which he operates, the community ensures that its resources are brought into play and not hoarded for speculative gain. Moreover, at one fell stroke the economic playing field is levelled, for those with valuable land pay more, and those with poor land, little or nothing.

What is proposed is not a gimmick; it is simply a return to the natural mode of raising revenue for the State, and *The Trial of Chaka Dlamini* has been written to open up this vision for all South Africans.

Johannesburg
July 1990

ACKNOWLEDGEMENTS

It was Peter Rose who first taxed us with the task of writing this book. Peter also made valuable comments on the early drafts, and encouraged the particular style we have adopted.

Of the many people who have had a hand in this book, our wives and families are owed a debt of gratitude, not only for putting up with it over the years it has taken to write, but also for the assistance and support given. Mary Cost and Karin Joseph bore the brunt of the typing, and Karin's ability to translate Mary's diskettes from Wordstar to Word Perfect was invaluable help. Libby Husemeyer, who edited the manuscript, made valuable comments on both content and style. To her we are extremely grateful, as we are to Frances Kendall who first suggested that we use Libby's expertise. Frances has also made other valuable suggestions which have contributed to the overall professionalism of the book.

Finally, we owe a great deal to the many people who read the manuscript and who commented on both the content and the philosophy.

1   CHAKA'S TRIAL

Ex Africa aliquid semper novi. (Out of Africa always something new.)
Pliny.

They came for him at about four in the morning. When he heard the heavy knock and saw the time on his old Wesclox Chaka thought it was the police, but he climbed out of bed, switched on a light and opened the door quietly and fearlessly.

There were four youths standing on the pathway.

"Dlamini," said the first boy, "you must come to Tshuma's house. We have come to fetch you."

Chaka knew it was senseless to argue, especially with these young messengers. He said he would put on some clothes and disappeared back into the house.

"Why is he not afraid?" asked the second boy.

"This is Chaka Dlamini," replied the first boy. "He is afraid of nothing."

Chaka came out a few minutes later, closed the door, and the five walked quickly away.

When they arrived at Tshuma's house, there was a gathering of about twenty youths crowded into the main room of the house. He knew at least three of them: Dabulamanzi, a student leader at Wits University; Wilson Radebe, an up-and-coming young banker and an assistant manager at his bank's Soweto branch; and Alfred Nkosi, a cameraman at the SABC. Was this some sort of court? thought Chaka. But surely not with people like Wilson and Alfred here. His thoughts were soon interrupted by Tshuma.

"Dlamini," he said, "you have been talking to some of our young men and some people think you are a bad influence on them. You give these men strange ideas about politics and economics, and they think that getting fancy jobs in Jo'burg will do more to advance our people than fighting the Boers. You talk to people about your systems of taxation and some people are starting to believe

1

you. But some of us think that you are nothing but a collaborator with the white capitalists. If they believed you and then put in your system, they would say that a black man thought up this thing. Then they would still keep everything and if we complained they would say that we gave them this system so why are we complaining? But I tell you, Dlamini, when the black people take power in Azania, the land will be redistributed to our people because it is rightfully theirs.

"And another thing: when our people commemorate days that are important to us, you sit in your house and drink beer and talk to boys about these ideas of yours. Maybe you are too old to go to meetings, but why do you stop these boys from going? Tell me, Dlamini: you are a man of influence — why do you not help our people fight the Boers instead of filling their heads with rubbish?

"But others say No, we must listen to you. So that is why we have brought you here, so you can talk to all of us, and then we can decide whether your ideas are worth listening to. So speak, Mdala, we are waiting for you."

"Tshuma," replied Chaka, "you flatter me by saying that I am a man of influence. The very fact that you have brought me here so early in the morning flatters me, because I am an ordinary man who, like millions of others, wants nothing more than to see our people take their rightful place in our country. Perhaps I am more fortunate than others because in my younger days I was able to travel to other countries, and I read books and spoke to people of many different nations. And perhaps because of that I saw something that many people who are locked up in these townships do not see."

"What can you see that we cannot see, Dlamini?"

"What I can see is that all these troubles are not new. We think that our troubles are unique; that they are all due to apartheid, which is unique to South Africa. But do you know that before the Russian revolution, the great Russian writer Leo Tolstoy was writing to his friend's son, the Czar's prime minister, Stolypin, urging him to free the people from taxes and to free the land for all. He knew this was the only way to stop the growing unrest and bring about real freedom. But Stolypin's answer was to hang more and more people until they called the hangman's noose 'Stolypin's necktie', and in the end Stolypin and the Czar were overwhelmed by the revolution. But did the peasants gain their freedom? Is Russia free today?

"And what about the French Revolution? Did you know that King Louis XVI's finance minister, Turgot, tried to replace all taxes with the 'impot unique' or single tax on land? But through their greed the aristocracy and the clergy refused to institute such reforms. Their heads were chopped off by the guillotine, but, at the end of the day, after the Revolution and Napoleon, did the peasants or France gain their freedom? It has taken France two hundred years to recover from the revolution. Some cynics would say that it has still not

2

recovered, for they ask, 'Is France any closer to ending poverty?'

"And what about the Iranian revolution? The Shah ruled the country with an iron rod in one hand and gifts in the form of social reforms in the other hand. But it was not enough to quell the unrest and the Ayatollah Khomeini came back to the country in triumph and to great adulation from the people. But the misery continued. As many people died at the hands of the new regime as died at the hands of the old."

"Dlamini, what is the point of all this history? We have no time to waste on those who stand in the way of the Struggle. All obstacles will be eliminated."

"Well, for one thing, Tshuma, social and political reforms are all very well, but they are not enough. Louis XVI and his tricameral parliament tried them and were guillotined for their trouble; the Russian Czar tried them and was brutally murdered; the Shah more than any of them made sweeping social and educational reforms, and look what happened to him."

"Don't worry, Dlamini, we mean business. We want power to the people, not just social reforms. And of course we want economic reform. Haven't you read the Freedom Charter? Is that not right, Comrades?"

The crowd answered Tshuma with a roar: "We want freedom! jobs! money! houses!" The cacophony poured forth until Tshuma asserted his authority and silenced them.

"Exactly," continued Chaka. "And this brings me to the real point. The people say they want freedom — but what is freedom? The peasants in Russia and France thought they would get freedom when they overthrew the monarchy, and the people of Iran thought they would get freedom when they got rid of the Shah. But the bloody revolutions and wars that followed didn't do them any good. The people bore the brunt of the fighting and dying, and in the end they were worse off than before.

"So the point, Tshuma, is that violent revolutions that replace one oppressor with another are no good. And this is exactly what many of our so-called friends overseas want us to do: have a violent revolution to replace apartheid with the same Marxist mish-mash that has enslaved and impoverished the people and the land in eastern Europe, China, Latin America and Africa. For a revolution to truly succeed, oppression must be replaced by a system based on the truth about Man. And in truth, both Man and land are free.

"What we want here in Africa is something truly radical, a real revolution of ideas that goes to the heart of the problem. We need to be free as much from the failings of capitalism as from the catastrophe of communism. I must speak to my people when I see them in danger of being enslaved by old ideas from overseas. I would rather die than be silent and let you lose the chance of real freedom. If I accepted capitalism or communism when I knew of their dangers, then I would indeed be a sell-out and an Uncle Tom."

3

"Is that what you call us, Dlamini?" cried Tshuma, angrily raising his right arm.

"No, let him speak, brother," said a voice from the crowd which Chaka recognised as that of Dabulamanzi. This time the crowd, which was strangely quiet, seemed to support Dabulamanzi, so Tshuma backed down.

"Very well then," he said, "tell us of your radical revolution."

"Do you know which of our people have already got their freedom in spite of apartheid and all the laws we have to put up with? It's the taxi owners, the hawkers, the spaza shop owners, the shebeen owners. And why? Because they have economic freedom. The government is going frantic trying to think of a way to tax the taxi owners and the best method they can think of is to raise the price of petrol. But if this government applied all the tax laws that apply to white businesses to the taxi owners and spaza shops, like PAYE, income tax, UIF, GST, and the rest, those businesses would close down in five minutes.

"Can you imagine Mbezi over there, who runs a shebeen near my house, deducting tax from the wages he pays to the people who work for him and then filling in the forms to pay this money to the Receiver of Revenue every month, balancing all this tax at the end of the year and then giving all his people little certificates so they can fill in more forms for the Receiver? You can laugh, my friends, but that is what the white people do, and that is what they want you to do as well. That is what they call the sophisticated first-world economy, and they want you to be part of this economy so that you will stop throwing stones at buses. You must get jobs like the white people and run businesses like them, and pay taxes like them.

"In the meantime, the taxi owners and so on are running successful businesses without all this nonsense. But I think you would agree that if every business, including the white businesses, ran like that, the government would get no tax and there would be no hospitals or roads or schools.

"So there is a problem, Tshuma. On the one hand, many of our people are breaking free through their own hard work in their own businesses, and the more this happens the better. When our people are economically free, political freedom will follow naturally.

"But on the other hand, the community must get its money in a fair way. This is what I talk to my friends about. How can this be done, without all the stupidities that the whites have dreamt up?"

"Dlamini, you are a clever old goat. I can see that some of these people here even agree with what you are saying. So tell us how you think it can be done."

"Tshuma, we have a strange thing here. You and your comrades see free enterprise as part of apartheid, but our brothers and sisters who are taxi owners or shebeen owners or hawkers are true examples of free enterprise. They didn't have to ask some government official if they could start their businesses; they don't have to comply with a lot of regulations to stay in business, and they don't

4

pay much tax. And that, Tshuma, is the secret. No taxes. For true freedom means freedom from taxes.

"The socialists tell you to grab power, tax the rich, let the State control the economy and then everybody will be free and wealthy. But we all know that wherever that has been tried, especially in Africa, the result has been the exact opposite. So the question I ask you is, why do our friends from overseas tell us to go for a people's revolution which, if it succeeds, will make us poorer and less free than we already are now? Especially if there is something else we can do? Well, you ask, what is that something else? My friends, I can see that you mean business, so I must answer your questions. And I do so willingly, not because I am frightened or want to defy you, but because I feel a strange compulsion to speak what seems to be for the good of my brothers and sisters. Also I see that although you are tough and ready to fight, you also want real answers to these questions.

"This then is my message to my people: we must free ourselves from the whole rotten mess of taxes which prevent many of us from finding work and which penalise all who work. And we must forget about foreign ideas that make many people favour the nationalisation of mines and banks, industry and land, and meddling by civil servants with the production of goods and services.

"Instead we must pay, and our government must collect, the natural rent on land. Everyone who has land, whether peasant or panel-beater, mining magnate or manufacturer, shopkeeper or shoemaker, must pay an annual rate according to the value of his or her land. If it is land with gold, perhaps he will have to pay millions; if it is land in Eloff Street, perhaps hundreds of thousands; if his land is in the platteland or the homelands, perhaps he will pay nothing. Remember, it is the people of South Africa, black and white, who over the centuries have given to every square inch of our country the value that it now has. The man who works well and hard on good land will make more than the man who works equally well on poor land. That 'more' is the people's because it is the natural rent arising out of the difference in the value of the land. Let me give you an example.

"Why does Mbezi run a successful shebeen? Those of you who drink there know some of the answers: he knows his business; he charges fair prices; his place is clean and well run; the people who work for him work hard but he treats them fairly. That is part of the answer, the part that has to do with the ability and work of Mbezi. The white man's tax system says that that ability must be taxed; my friends, I say that is unfair.

"But there is another reason why he is successful: he is in a good part of Soweto. Not the best, but good. People there have good homes, some have bought their houses and most are thinking about doing that. Because of the doctors, lawyers and other professionals from the neighbourhood who have a drink there, it has become known as a high-class tavern. Move Mbezi to some

5

other part of Soweto that is not as prosperous as this part, or to a far-off country village, and with all his ability and hard work he would not be as successful. So some of his success is due to his own efforts and some is due to where he is. And that is the part the community should look to for its revenue. The problem is, how do you calculate it?

"So you see, Tshuma, there are many questions but not so many answers. But this we do know: our people are beginning to shake off the yoke of apartheid by getting economic freedom. Apartheid will die, but something almost as bad can come in its place: the white man's tax system. It strangles the economy of this country like a giant python, and it will also strangle our brothers and sisters who are starting to find their freedom through their small businesses, if the same system is applied to them.

"We need to see for ourselves and show all others that out of Africa can come a new freedom. We think that we will be free when apartheid is destroyed. That, my friends, is a fallacy. Apartheid will go one way or another, but that does not mean that we will be free when that day comes. For freedom to be real we must all have economic freedom, the freedom that Mbezi and hundreds of others have achieved. If we can convince the white man that this is true economic freedom, then perhaps we shall free him as well."

At this a young man leapt to his feet and started shouting:

"Tshuma, this man Dlamini is a capitalist collaborator. He can't fool us with his fancy words. Of course the taxi owners and the spaza shops are successful; it's because they operate in this capitalist apartheid system which is unnatural and unjust. But in a proper socialist system they won't be necessary; we will have a transport system that will charge much less than the taxis and we will have co-operative shops that are much more efficient and cheaper than the spaza shops. A handful of people will not be able to exploit the majority like the taxi owners are doing now. This Chaka Dlamini is guilty of all the things you said he was guilty of. Why must we listen to any more of his rubbish?"

"No, comrade, we must listen to him," called a voice from the crowd. "He has a point of view that nobody else has: not the socialists or the capitalists."

To Chaka's great surprise, it was Dabulamanzi who had spoken up for him yet again. But Dabulamanzi commanded some respect in this company. He stepped forward then and turned to address the others.

"We despise capitalism," he said, "because we see it as a stooge of apartheid, and therefore we say that socialism is right because it is the opposite of capitalism. But Chaka says there is a third way, and I think we should listen to him. Petrus has just said that under socialism the taxi drivers won't rob the people. Under socialism the taxi drivers will work for the state and will charge fares that are laid down by the state and go where the state tells them to go. Is that better than the system we have now? I don't think so. Under Petrus' system the taxi drivers will go on routes even if nobody wants to go there, or they will

6

say that the taxi is broken; why should they care? They will still get their money from the state but I don't think the people will have a very good transport system.

"I am not saying that Chaka is right, but I am saying that he has something to tell us. Let us listen to him before we pass judgement on him."

A murmur of assent went round the room, and Petrus nodded reluctantly.

So began, even that very day, in the tiny front room of Tshuma's house, Chaka's discussions and conversations with the people in the townships. This was to be Chaka's trial, by the people for the people.

2   FREE LAND

*And God said, let us make man in our image... and let them have dominion... over all the
earth.*
                                                                    Genesis 1:26

Whatever lives is full of the Lord. Claim nothing; enjoy, do not covet His property.
                                        Eesha Upanishad. W B Yeats transl.

"Dlamini," said Petrus, "Dabulamanzi says that you don't believe
in capitalism or socialism, but in some third way. What is
this third way?"

"Petrus, capital and labour are really part of the same thing. Some people
think that capital is the more important, some think labour is more important,
but both are necessary to produce wealth. Take the example of Mbezi and his
shebeen that I was talking of earlier. What is the first thing he needs to start up
his business?"

"You said that his site was important, and I agree: he must first have
somewhere to set up his shebeen."

"That's right, Dabulamanzi." said Chaka. "The first thing is land — but
not just any land. In Mbezi's case it must be where his customers are, and they
are not in the middle of the Karoo! What is the next thing he needs?"

Dabulamanzi, who had just passed Economics I at university, thought
about his answer before replying hesitantly:

"I'm not sure what my economics lecturers would say, but I think that he
needs the right size room, tables and chairs, a good music system, glasses, a
fridge, money to buy his first supply of liquor, money to pay wages. I guess they
would call this capital."

"Very good. Now what else would he need?"

"He would need people to work for him — labour. Ah," he exclaimed
suddenly, "so that is what you are getting at — the three factors of production:

8

land, labour and capital."

"Correct. So you see, my friends, the capitalists say that capital is the most important thing for a business and therefore the man who owns the capital must own and control the business. The socialists say no, labour is more important and therefore labour must control the means of production. And while these two dogs are fighting over the bone, the landowner comes in quietly and takes the bone for himself. Sometimes I wonder if capital and labour have even noticed that the bone has been taken from under their noses.

"You see, land is so obvious that everyone ignores it. But it is fundamental to man's most basic right, the right to live. And to live a man must work, and work must be based on land. It is truly the first factor of production because everything we have comes from the earth, and is modified by labour with the help of capital.

"For example, take a man who lives on a small piece of land and grows food for his family. The land, under the tribal system of our fathers, is granted to him by the chief or headman and usually he has tenure for the whole of his life. His capital is his spade or hoe or plough, perhaps some oxen to pull the plough; labour is supplied by himself and his family. From this comes his wealth: food for his family and money from the surplus food he can sell and then exchange for clothes, matches, blankets and so on. Wealth cannot be produced by land alone, or labour alone, or capital alone.

"But labour and capital in themselves will not necessarily determine how wealthy or successful a man will be. A business like Mbezi's can have the prettiest and most efficient waitresses, the most comfortable chairs, the best music and the widest selection of liquor, but if it is in the wrong place it will not be as successful as a shebeen that has all these things, but is in the right place. In Sotho they say, *motho ke motho ka batho* — whatever a man is, he is on account of other people. So it is with land: its value is on account of other people, and he has the right to that land because other people allow him that right."

At that moment there was a commotion in the street outside and a young girl burst into the house. Chaka recognised her as Dabulamanzi's girl friend, Nonquase.

"You must all go," she said. "The police have heard that there is a people's court and they are searching the township."

"Where do the cops get these stories?" asked Tshuma, irritated by the interruption. "But I suppose we must all go. And Dlamini, remember: we still need to hear plenty more from you. Dabulamanzi and Petrus, you go with him to his house."

So Chaka and the two young men hurriedly left the house as the others dispersed in various directions.

Dabulamanzi and Petrus were keen to continue the discussion when they arrived at Chaka's house, but not before they had helped themselves to some of

9

Chaka's never-ending supply of beer. Chaka smiled to himself; he always kept plenty of beer on hand for his young friends and Dabulamanzi knew exactly where to go to help himself. Petrus looked very comfortable and at home lounging on Chaka's modest sofa with a can of Castle in his hand.

"Chaka," said Petrus, "I still don't know what you are getting at. You talk about land as a factor of production and about the importance of the position of the site for a business, but so what? Is land more important than labour?"

"Petrus, every single thing that Man must do, everything that he eats, wears, lives in, rides on, his whole physical existence depends on land. It is as important to him as the water he drinks, the sun that lights his way, and the air he breathes. Without access to land a Man cannot work, and without work he cannot live like a Man; he must then depend on others and if he has to depend on others they will treat him not as a man but as something inferior, something that must be told what to do, where to live, what to eat and wear. It is then a small step to rob him of political rights, and then he is no better than a slave, whether he is called that or not."

"Okay, I get your point. We know all that, but the Freedom Charter addresses those problems. Is your solution any different?"

"Petrus, you are a socialist; tell me, what is your policy in regard to land? What would you do if you were running the country?"

"Well, the Freedom Charter is fairly straightforward on this point. It says that restriction of land ownership on a racial basis shall be ended, and all the land re-divided amongst those who work it, to banish famine and hunger. Then it says that all shall have the right to occupy land wherever they choose and also that all people shall have the right to live where they choose."[1]

"Comrade, I must compliment you on your knowledge of the Freedom Charter," said Dabulamanzi.

"Everyone should know the Freedom Charter," retorted Petrus. "I can recite the whole Charter."

Chaka intervened quickly before the discussion got completely side-tracked. These young men loved to spend hours impressing anyone who cared to listen with their fluent recitations of the Charter. Whether they understood it was another matter.

"Right, Petrus, that is what the Charter says. How do you see this in practical terms? Would you say that the Charter meets the need for free land?"

"Absolutely. The Charter says that all shall have the right to occupy the land wherever they choose. And all the land shall be re-divided amongst those who work the land. Surely that is what free land is all about?"

"Wait a minute," interrupted Dabulamanzi. "I have heard Chaka talk about free land before. I'm not sure that I understand what he means, but I am sure that he does not mean that the land will be free — in the same way that free market people don't mean that when you go to the market your fruit and vegetables will be free. They mean that all markets should be free of any restrictions, and then, they say, the market will work best. That I can understand, even if I don't necessarily agree with it. But free land, that is a bit more difficult to understand."

"You are right, Dabulamanzi," replied Chaka, "free land is difficult to understand. We talk loosely about free people, free trade, free markets and free land, but the one common factor is responsibility or duty, and duty regrettably is the one thing nobody likes to talk about. It is sort of taken for granted, like in the Freedom Charter. I cannot recite the Charter as Petrus can, but from what I remember, the word responsibility, or the idea which this word embodies, is not mentioned at all. Yes, I know, Petrus, we could debate that point for another week, and perhaps we shall sometime, but I only bring up the subject to explain what I mean by free land.

"In a democracy like the United Kingdom, the people are relatively free because they observe, by and large, the three great duties required of people living in society: the duties not to injure another, not to defame another, and not unlawfully to imprison another. Normally these duties are turned around and spoken of as rights, but when you think about it, it is the duties that are carried out a thousand times a day, and the rights are only thought about when someone does not do their duty. It is the same with free markets: they will work only when people realise their duties and do not abuse the privileges inherent in a free market. The free market people will say that if there are abuses, the market will no longer be free. Maybe; but I think they should spell out the duties that go with a free market a lot more clearly than they do.

"So what are the duties that go with free land? There are three for the individual who has a piece of land, and three for the authorities in respect of all the land in their care. The three duties for the individual are that he must keep his land in good condition, must not disturb his neighbours' enjoyment of their land, and he must pay the rent. The authorities' duties are that they must keep unoccupied land in good condition, they must make unoccupied land available to anyone who wishes to use it, and finally, they must collect the rent. So you see, Petrus, that is not far from what the Charter says, only I have put the emphasis on duties, whereas the Charter puts it on rights."

The two young men had just got up to get themselves another beer when there was a knock on the door. Petrus and Dabulamanzi immediately made for the back door but Chaka shouted at them to stay. "It is only Nonquase and Wilson Radebe. Bring them some beer."

Dabulamanzi and Petrus came back into the living room looking rather sheepish, and Dabulamanzi said defiantly: "That's what apartheid has done to us; we are even afraid to be seen talking and drinking with our friends."

"It is as I said," replied Chaka. "When man's basic right to the land is taken away, any sort of evil or distortion can happen. Apartheid is one of the guises it adopts in South Africa at this time. But I am forgetting my manners. Nonquase and Wilson, welcome to my home."

"I don't have to guess what you are talking about," said Nonquase. "The only thing Dabulamanzi ever talks about is politics. Politics for breakfast, politics for lunch, politics for supper, politics to go to sleep to. So I am right, am I not? You are talking about politics and as usual not doing anything about it."

"You are only partly right, Nonquase," said Chaka. "We are really talking about economics, but the two are very closely linked."

"And equally boring."

"No, Nonquase," said Dabulamanzi. "You must listen, but first tell us what happened at Tshuma's house after we left."

"By the time the police arrived everyone but Tshuma and his girlfriend, Gladys, had left. I went to the Gumedes' house across the road and I saw the police go into Tshuma's house. They were there quite a long time, and when they came out they took Tshuma with them. When the police had gone I went to his house; Gladys was crying and saying that Tshuma had been arrested. The place was a terrible mess, papers everywhere. So I helped Gladys tidy up and while we were doing that Wilson came in and helped also. Then we came here to find you and tell you what has happened."

While Nonquase talked, Petrus had felt the familiar old rage welling in him again. "I suppose, Dlamini," he burst out now in a voice dripping with bitter sarcasm, "that policemen just coming into our houses as if that is their God-given right, and detaining anyone they like, or rather, don't like, for as long as they feel is necessary, is also due to your stupid ideas on rights to land."

Petrus threw his empty beer can to the ground and crushed it with his foot with all the anger and frustration he could muster. "The only way to deal with these people is the way they know: violence. And they say we must give up violence. They make me sick."

"Petrus, it is ignorance of the basic principles I have been speaking about which is behind these problems. If you try to correct a wrong which is just a result of ignoring fundamental principles, nothing will really change. Sure, you may correct that particular wrong, but another will soon pop up in its place. As I said to you before, if you deny some men free access to land, you deny them their very right to life. And from that a whole multitude of wrongs will spring."

"Okay, okay," shouted Petrus, "stop giving us fine words that mean nothing and start giving us answers."

Wilson, who'd been listening quietly, nodded in agreement with Petrus' outburst and said, "Petrus does have a point, Chaka. These are fine words indeed that you speak, but what do they mean in a practical sense?"

Now I'm really on trial, thought Chaka as he looked at the four pairs of angry eyes challenging him to respond. The meeting at Tshuma's house earlier that morning had been easy for him, but now the time had come for real answers.

"Before you and Nonquase came in, Wilson, we spoke of the duties that go with the occupation of land. One of those duties is to pay the natural rent. What is this rent? It is the benefit the owner derives from occupying better land, and since it is the community that determines which land is superior to other land, this natural rent is due to the community. Imagine that one man owned all the land; he would still let others use it, but he would charge them for the use of each piece of land. We call that rent. Natural rent is based on the same principle, except that although the land does not belong to the community, and individuals have title deeds which give them unrestricted use of their land for as long as they want it, the difference in the value between the least productive piece of land in use and all the others, is due to the community."

"Tell me, Chaka," asked Wilson, "how does the community decide whether one piece of land is better than another? You could have a whole army of bureaucrats fighting about that one."

"The short answer to that, Wilson, is that 'the community' is determining relative values all the time by means of market prices paid for land. As you know, there are enormous differences in the value of land. An acre of land in the middle of Johannesburg will sell for more than R40 million, while in the far north-western Cape, you would be lucky to get R40 an acre. So the natural rent or usage charge for land in the middle of Johannesburg would be far greater than the charge for land in the Kalahari, because, as the market values tell us, the one may be as much as a million times more productive than the other.

"To sum up, to whatever land man has the right of access, he has it on account of other people. Not only do they agree not to take away his land or its produce, but his land also enjoys many things other people have done over the years, such as build roads, bridges, railways, airports or large cities. Even if his land was bare it would be just as valuable according to how much his land benefited from these things. For by definition all land values, I mean of ground only, not the buildings and other improvements on it, are wholly and entirely due to the work and development of the community over the years. Whatever land a man has, its unimproved value is on account of other people.

"This account must, therefore, be settled — not with another man, but with Mankind, to whom the Maker has given dominion over all the earth. And as the family is the unit of the nation, so the nation is the unit of Man. Therefore, in practical terms, this account must be settled with the nation — the community, the people. It is the community that provides benefits to the landowner, and therefore it is only a matter of common sense that he should pay the community for them.

"Moreover, so long as he settles the account for his land, no one — least of all a tax collector — should have the right to take from what is left of his production, for that is the fruit of his labour. Tax on work of any form, whether

13

labour, management, enterprise or research, is not merely lacking in common sense, it is counter-productive and unjust.

"But all this is ignored in our country's tax structure. The people in the remote rural areas are subject to the same high levels of tax as people in the cities. The labour and capital used in the marginal rural areas could never produce the same amount of wealth as the same labour and capital could produce in the cities. Therefore any taxes charged in the marginal areas would make their earnings unacceptably low.

"So what do people in these areas do? They come flooding into the towns to seek, not so much a fortune, but simple survival. But nobody says that these shanty towns around the cities are due to taxes on the marginal areas; no, they will dream up all sorts of other reasons, like the drought, the homelands policy, apartheid. The simple truth is that if you ignore the natural rent that is due to the community, all sorts of distortions must occur. Taxes become more and more complex and punitive, and the more punitive they become, the greater the economic distortion in remote areas which are normally the margin of economic activity."

Chaka broke off his discourse at this point, excused himself and disappeared into the kitchen to put the kettle on for tea. While he was away, his young listeners, including Petrus, were silent and thoughtful. Chaka had indeed given some real answers, but it was more than they could digest at once.

When Chaka returned with the tea tray, Wilson felt brave enough to put a question to him. "Chaka, I think that we all agree that the government, or the community if you like, must have a share of the wealth produced so that it can maintain things like hospitals and schools and a police force and so on. But you maintain that the taxes today cause distortions in the production of wealth and so, if I follow your reasoning, you would do away with taxes and have a user charge on land instead. And that user charge would be based on the relative value of the land. But is there really a difference, other than the way the money is collected? I'm sure your user charge would be almost as difficult to collect as taxes are. The tax system has some problems, sure, but by and large it seems pretty efficient to me. Do you really think it is that bad?"

"Well," replied Chaka, "as you well know, I'm no expert on tax, but I shall tell you of a visit I made to my friend Robert Armitage one Sunday about a year ago. My friend Solly Kgamphe drove me there and we had Sunday lunch on the terrace and drank beer and wine. It was very nice, you know. Solly really enjoyed himself; he even had a swim in the swimming pool and now I think he dreams of the day when he can have a pool in his garden."

"Dlamini," said Petrus, irritated again, "cut out all this white capitalist rubbish. Is there any point to your story?"

"Oh yes, there's a point," smiled Chaka, "But it's a long story. Pour the tea, Nonquase, and I'll tell it to you."

14

3   THE MAD TAXER'S TEA PARTY

Here lies the father of taxation,
May Heaven, his faults forgiving,
Grant him repose which he, while living,
Would never give the Nation.
    Epitaph of Jean Baptiste Colbert,
    Minister of Finance to Louis XIV

Well, as I was saying, my friend Solly drove me to Robert's house in the northern suburbs of Johannesburg. We sat and drank tea and then beer, then had lunch with wine, then more tea, and all the time we talked and talked. Somebody called our party the mad taxer's tea party. Two of Robert's economist friends were there, Michael Barnes and Anthony van der Merwe.

"Chaka," said Robert, "I found a quote that you'll enjoy."
He read it out to us:
If one were to set out with a specific, stated objective of designing a tax system which would act as the maximum disincentive to effort at all levels of society, which would penalise and deter thrift, energy and success, it would be almost impossible to do better than the one we have in this country today.[1]
"Who said that? Chaka Dlamini?" asked Solly.
"Good guess," said Robert, "but actually it was Lord Soames, the last governor of Rhodesia. Lord Soames was complaining about the U.K. tax system at a time when he and Mrs Thatcher sat on the opposition benches. I wonder if he could say after a decade of Conservative rule that the situation is any better? Unlikely, I would guess. But never mind the U.K. tax system, do you think it also applies to ours, Michael?"
"Most definitely," replied Michael. But before he could go on, Anthony interrupted.
"I don't agree. I think we have an extremely well-balanced and

sophisticated tax system. For a small, almost third-world country, we have an unbelievable depth of expertise in tax matters. And in this country, unlike many others, the people who make a living advising clients how to minimise their tax liabilities also advise the government on tax matters. The Margo Commission,[2] for example, relied very heavily on tax consultants."

"With due respect, Anthony, the Commission didn't get very far. How many of its proposals have been accepted? Tax consultants have a lot to answer for in this country. Okay, they're just businessmen doing their job, but when they help their clients to avoid taxes, they help foster the notion that our tax system is a method of robbing the poor to pay the rich."

"Please explain, Michael," I asked. "How can the tax system possibly rob the poor to pay the rich?"

"Chaka, it obviously doesn't do that directly, but take schemes like the old film partnership scheme and the bloodstock scheme. To put it simply, wealthy people invest in these and because of the generous allowances they receive for tax purposes, they will pay little or no tax. They may be lucky and make money out of their investment, but even if they don't, the money they lose will be considerably less than the tax they would have paid. These schemes are obviously not open to any but the wealthy, and if you're an ordinary bloke working like a devil to survive and still have a compulsory non-refundable deduction from your wages every month, and you are hit with GST on nearly everything you buy, you'll probably feel less than thrilled to learn that many wealthy people pay little or no tax on their income.

"Tax consultants are the ones who organise these schemes, and while they may be perfectly legal, I think they should look further than their clients' interests to the impact these schemes have on inter-group relationships. Many a revolution has been caused by the fact that the haves pay little or no tax while the have-nots pay through the nose."

"Okay, Michael," said Robert, "but tax consultants are really a side issue. Can we get back to Lord Soames? What really is wrong with our tax system?"

"Well, let's look at the components of the system. First there is income tax, then there is expenditure tax, so they get you both ways. Income tax is really very simple: you pay tax on your earnings less any allowable deductions. The complications arise when you try to define income and expenditure. Probably the best known book on tax in South Africa is Silke. This book spends about 300 pages on income and another 250 or so on deductions and there are still hundreds of cases every year where taxpayers dispute the Receiver's ruling on what is or is not income or expenditure.

"The real problem is that people who earn money have a belief that it is theirs, and so they see taxation as some kind of robbery. Then they fight tooth and nail to keep what they feel is rightfully theirs. This is where tax consultants come in. But as I said earlier, if you're an ordinary salaried employee earning under the SITE[3] limits you don't have much scope for avoiding tax. In fact, as far as the tax man is concerned, you aren't even part of the tax system because you don't have to fill in a tax return."

"Stop there for a moment, Michael," I said; "are you saying that income tax contains the seeds of its own destruction?"

"It most certainly does. The harder one works, the more efficient, productive, inventive, profitable and so on one is, the more one is taxed. So then comes the theory that these inventive, hard-working people mustn't be over-taxed because they're the ones that drive the economy, create jobs and the rest; we must spread the tax to everyone, and then we'll be able to relieve these talented people of their terrible tax burden. So then the government slaps on expenditure taxes like GST. But a lot of people make a fortune out of GST so then they say that VAT[2] will be fairer because it will be more difficult to evade. But because it's so complex, we must tax everything, including food. But what about the poor? Give them food coupons, they say. And so this whole tottering structure is added to and added to until one day it will collapse under its own weight."

"Very good, but why is there this fixation with income tax?" I asked.

"I believe," said Michael, "that there are two basic reasons why income tax started the rot. Firstly, it is a misinterpretation of Adam Smith's first maxim of taxation. He said that the subjects of every state ought to contribute towards the support of the government, as nearly as possible, in proportion to their respective abilities; that is, he went on to say, in proportion to the revenue which they respectively enjoy under the protection of the state. Now I believe that 'revenue' has been misinterpreted as income, and 'ability' as the amount of income. In other words, this is interpreted as meaning the more you earn, the greater your ability to pay tax. This is a fallacy which has never been seriously challenged.

"The second problem is that many people think income is easy to measure, whereas in fact it is virtually impossible to measure. Yet income tax came to be accepted, and everyone thought that its principles were written in stone."

"May I be devil's advocate once again?" said Anthony. "Surely that is right: the more you earn, the more tax you should pay. Earnings are indeed a measure of ability to pay tax. How else are you going to measure, in a fairly precise way, how tax should be calculated? I grant that it can become pretty complicated, but so what? We have, as I said, a vast array of tax expertise, and huge computers to do all the work. And at least income tax is based on hard facts, not some airy fairy theory about one man's ability versus another's. And, let me remind you, Adam Smith himself said that the tax ought to be certain, and not arbitrary."

"Ah yes, Anthony," replied Michael, the resident expert on Adam Smith, "but he also said that the quantity to be paid ought to be clear and plain to the contributor, and to every other person. Where it is not, he said, the taxpayer is in the power of the tax man — and, I might add, the tax consultant."

"Yes," said Anthony, "but you must agree that income is a measure of ability."

"No I don't. A given amount of labour and capital employed in a marginal area can never produce the same wealth that a similar amount of labour and capital would produce in a prime area. Ability, in the sense meant by Adam Smith, is determined by location — the revenue which they respectively enjoy under the protection of the state is how Adam Smith put it. And protection here means things like infrastructure, density of population, closeness to markets, not only security. The person in the marginal area would have to double or treble his labour and capital to produce the same wealth as the person on the prime site. And then what would happen to him? His tax on employment would shoot up, and his return on capital would become unacceptable. And on top of that he would have to pay the same amount of income tax. This is what Lord Soames was talking about: the tax system is a disincentive to effort."

"Well, okay," said Anthony, reluctant to concede any points. "But I can't agree that tax on employment, as you put it, has anything to do with the employer. That is the tax paid by the employee on his salary or wages, and is not paid by the employer."

"Well, let's go back to Adam Smith then. He said that the level of wages depended on two things: the demand for labour and the price of provisions. If these two conditions remained the same, a tax on wages would have the effect of raising the wage to the position where the worker's take-home pay left him in the same position as before. In other words, the tax would really be paid by the employer; in fact, the employer would have to pay not just the tax, but something extra as well. For example, if the worker was paid R100 a week, and then a tax of 20% was imposed, the employer would have to pay him an extra R25 a week in order to give him a take-home pay of R100. This R25 would inevitably be passed on to the consumer. Adam Smith blamed the decline of industry and the increase in unemployment on such a tax.

"So what Smith is saying, really, is that the gross wage is a meaningless figure. The net take-home pay must satisfy the worker's minimum requirements in terms of food, shelter, clothing, transport, entertainment and so on; if it doesn't, then he will demand more. Whether he gets it, of course, will depend on the demand for his particular skills. This in turn will depend on the strength of demand, or lack of it, in the economy. The bottom line is that labour is not a valid target for taxation, and if it is taxed, this tax will cause distortions in the economy."

"Anthony, what do you make of Michael's argument?" I asked.

"Well," replied Anthony, as reluctantly as before, "his argument does have some valid points, I suppose. But the belief these days that everyone must make a contribution to the state's coffers is so strong that it would be extremely difficult to change it."

"Okay, Michael and Anthony," I said, "if I can summarise your arguments, it seems that if we accept that labour is a valid target for taxation, we must accept the enormous problems, not just for individual taxpayers but also for the economy as a whole, that go with such an idea. On the other hand, if labour is not a valid target for taxation, then what should replace it?"

"Right, now we come to the taxation of expenditure, or the so-called indirect taxes: GST, VAT, customs and excise duties, stamp duties, tax on bank transactions, and so on. What did Adam Smith say about them, Michael?" asked Robert.

"Sorry to interrupt once again," said Anthony, "but let me get in my two cents' worth before Michael gets carried away again. I'm all for these taxes. If you want a replacement for income tax, they're the answer. Indirect taxes spread the load; the rich pay more because they spend more, but everyone pays their fair share. Also, there are fewer collection points for the tax authorities to monitor — fewer than the millions of individual taxpayers anyway."

"With respect, Anthony, you've fallen into the same trap," replied Michael. "Wage earners can only pay these taxes out of their wages, and if wages are set at the least a wage earner will accept, given the demand for his labour and the price of commodities, then any such taxes will either create a demand for increased wages or will impoverish the wage earner if such a demand cannot be met. In fact, Adam Smith said that a tax on the 'necessaries of life' operates in the same manner as a direct tax upon the wages of labour. This tax must in the long run be paid by the employer, who will pass it on in the price of his goods, so that in the end the tax will be paid by the consumer.

"But I also want to deal with another aspect of indirect taxes. Anthony said that these taxes 'spread the load', and that is true. No matter where you are, if a pair of shoes is R100, you pay that plus whatever percentage for GST, and that is taken to be right and fair. But what is forgotten is that some areas, especially those operating at the margin of economic activity, are not able to bear even a half percent of tax.

"Let me tell you a story about the effect of such a tax. When the gold mines really started to produce, but had to go underground to find the gold, what the mine owners needed more than anything was labour. The obvious source was the local indigenous population. But why should they go and work on the mines? The work was heavy, the pay low, and they were living comfortably off their lands and cattle, which were plentiful in those days and which they would have had to leave in the hands of their wives and families for months on end.

"So the mine owners tried Chinese labour, but, as is well known, that didn't really work, and they were forced to go back to local labour again. But how to get them to leave their land? The mine owners were extremely

19

influential — Rhodes himself was prime minister of the Cape Colony — so they got the colonial governments in the Cape and Natal to impose duties on manufactured articles. These were the sort of things the local people had come to take for granted over the years, such as blankets, hoes, buckets, glass beads and so on. But the problem for the tribesmen was this: their economy was so delicately poised that any additional cost would upset it completely. If they wanted these things, the only answer was additional income, and the mine owners were waiting to give it to them. Just to make sure they moved, the colonial governments also imposed hut and poll taxes which forced them to look for jobs even if they didn't want these things."

"What, may I ask, has this to do with indirect taxes in this day and age?" Anthony was clearly irritated by Michael's long story.

"Why suddenly over the last ten years or so have we seen such a large influx of people to the cities? Why would people leave the relative peace and harmony of the rural areas to live in squatters' shacks near a major city? Obviously the slum must offer something better, but what? Sure, we have had droughts and crop failures and locust plagues, but this country has had them often before. And, I suppose, the dropping of influx control made it easier for people to move to the cities. Others say that the pressure of population forces people to leave areas that cannot support large numbers. All this may play a part, but to my mind, the major culprit is a tax system which grinds heaviest on those who can least afford it. There is no escape from an indirect tax except to move to an area that is not an area of marginal economic activity. The irony is that these indirect taxes which have forced the country folk to come to the cities were imposed by the government which, in terms of its homeland policy, wanted them to stay there and keep out of so-called white South Africa!"

"Michael," I asked, "that is the second time you have used the term 'area of marginal activity'. I'm not sure I understand what you mean."

"Chaka, very simply, it is the edge of economic activity beyond which a man will not go. For Anthony here, that may mean the Johannesburg CBD; he wouldn't even move to Benoni. But for a man in a rural area that area may be his margin. He earns enough to keep himself and his family and he is basically happy with his lot like the man in Goldsmith's *Deserted Village*:

> *A man he was to all the country dear,*
> *And passing rich with forty pounds a year;*
> *Remote from towns he ran his godly race,*
> *Nor e'er had changed, nor wished to change his place.*

"But impose a tax on him so that the forty pounds become thirty-nine, and he will be placed in a position he is not prepared to accept. At the margin of production there is no surplus — there is only enough to keep a person in the lowest state that he is prepared to accept. Many things can upset this balance, and some things like a drought or crop failure he will endure because he knows

20

that one day better times will come. But a tax he cannot fight."

"So, Michael," I said, "the gist of what you are saying is that the taxes we have today are a fundamental cause of our economic problems because they destroy economic activity at the margin of production. It would seem that if this continues, the margin will continue to shrink until we are left with vast areas of nothing and huge cities of teeming poverty-stricken masses."

"Absolutely," replied Michael, "and there are two problems which will ensure that this scenario will come about. The first is the belief that, as there is nothing fundamentally wrong with our tax system, we must have taxes. Since there will always be some people who will be hurt by taxes, tax reform therefore consists of hurting the fewest for the greatest common good. The second problem is that there is a strong belief that all this urbanisation is a good thing; the rural areas are good for nothing, and if people want help, the city is the place to get it. Well, if we want our cities to turn into second Rio de Janeiros or Sao Paulos, then we must just carry on. I find it hard to believe that is what we want, but that's the way we are going."

Robert came in at this point. "As soon as one moves away from the collection of the natural rent, the tax system must get more and more complicated, and distort the economy. Adam Smith tells the story of the bricked-up windows you can see in old houses in England. My wife and I went on a coach tour there some years ago, and the guide pointed out these windows, telling us that they were bricked up because of the window tax.

"Well, Adam Smith says that this tax started off as a hearth tax — you know, fireplaces. The tax collector could easily count the chimneys and assess the tax. Then when people got smart and linked several fireplaces to one chimney, the tax collector had to go into the houses to count the fireplaces, but you can imagine how popular that was — the Englishman's home is his castle and all that! So, after a few tax collectors had been beaten up and thrown out of the house, they decided to base the tax on the number of windows, which could be counted from the outside again. And, of course, on the old principle that if you tax something you diminish its quantity, windows were bricked up.

"I also remember something about an Egyptian pasha who thought that the millions of date palms growing alongside the Nile would be a good subject for taxation. And, on the same principle, many of the palms were chopped down, causing widespread starvation."

"Another thing that taxation diminishes," said Michael, "is morality. If people believe that the system of taxation is unfair, they won't worry too much about cheating the system a little. Obviously, statistics on tax evasion are non-existent, but estimates are fairly horrifying. I read an article which quoted estimates of $26 billion in lost taxes in the US, and that was in 1976! In Britain it was estimated that 7,5% of the GNP was not declared for tax purposes. And in the traditional 'black' economy countries like Italy and France, this percentage

21

is much higher.

"This article also quoted the results of public opinion surveys in Britain. In one survey respondents were given a list of so-called immoral activities and asked whether, in their opinion, such activities were 'wrong' or 'acceptable'. The vast majority — some 70%, if I remember correctly — thought that 'avoiding paying tax on money you earn in your spare time' was acceptable."[4]

"I'm surprised that the percentage was so low," chipped in Anthony. "I wonder how many people doing a private deal on a motor car pay the full GST. And I wonder if anyone pays GST on a private sale of a hi-fi set or a piano if the price is over R1 000. Precious few, I'll bet."

"So, gentlemen," asked Robert, "what is the solution?"

"That, my friend," I replied, "will have to wait for another day. The sun has sunk below the tree tops, but before you open yet another bottle of wine to celebrate the occasion, Solly and I must get back to Soweto. But think about it, because without a solution we become yet another bunch of complainers who never do anything."

"So, my friends, that is the story of my visit to my white friends in the northern suburbs, and I hope, Wilson, that it answers some of your questions about the tax system."

"It does, Chaka," replied Wilson, "but it doesn't answer the question of what should take its place."

"As you know, I don't think we should have taxes," said Chaka. "Taxes are robbery; there is no need for them. The community must get its money by charging for the benefits it supplies. No more, no less."

4   THE NEXT GREAT TREK
— FROM TAXES TO RENT

There is a sense in which all taxes are antagonistic to free enterprise... In my opinion, the least bad tax is the property tax on the unimproved value of land, proposed by Henry George long ago.

Milton Friedman

Render therefore unto Caesar the things which are Caesar's.
Luke 20:25

Wilson stared at Chaka quizzically. "Chaka, I have heard you say — today, in fact — that you would like to see the government collect its revenue by means of a user charge on site values. But is that really feasible? Taxes today raise over fifty billion rand and still the government has to raise more money by borrowing. Even if you could reduce that by getting rid of the cost of apartheid, and scale down the cost of so-called security, we are still talking about a lot of money."

"Chaka," chipped in Dabulamanzi, "you are just giving taxes another name; if the government collects money from people, that is a tax. What else can it be?"

"Dabulamanzi," said Chaka patiently, "I have said many times before that the natural rent on land — you remember how we put it earlier this morning, the benefit a person derives from occupying better land — is due to the community. I have suggested that this be collected by means of a site user charge — you can call it a tax if you like, but the word 'tax' implies a burden. I am not talking about a burden; I am talking about something that belongs to the community in the first place. The problem really is twofold: first, and most difficult, to get people to understand what the problem is; and then to collect what is due to the community."

23

"Okay, Chaka," said Wilson, "let's assume for the moment that you are talking sense. How would you start to implement such a system?"

"You are right to ask how one would start. The present system of taxation is so ingrained that any real reform would have to be done very gradually. So let us start from where we are. The tax system is made up of a number of different aspects. The main source of tax is from income tax on companies and individuals; then there are indirect taxes such as GST and customs and excise duties. Then we have a whole crowd of piffling little taxes such as the duty on bank transactions and stamps on contracts. Then there are the infamous Regional Services Council levies, and finally the local property taxes paid by whites.

"So let's start with income tax. Individuals pay the biggest chunk of all, and economists are worried because the tax rates for individuals are so high compared with the major industrial countries. In fact taxation, together with the political situation of course, is said to be the main reason for whites leaving the country. But if you recall the story I have just told you about my visit to Robert's house, you will remember that the level of wages is based on the demand for labour, the price of commodities, and the least a person is willing to accept.

"To an employer, that means the gross wages paid to his employees. But to the worker, it means the money he takes home after all deductions, the money he can spend on the things he needs. So to say that wages are a valid target for taxation is farcical. You could say to a worker who is getting a gross wage of R1 000 a month, but taking home R850, that his gross is to be increased to R3 000 a month but the tax is being increased to R2 150. What will he care?

"So the first thing I would do on this road to eliminating taxes is to do away with the tax on salaries and wages. This sounds like a major reform, but in fact it is only a small step. The employer would pay the tax — as he does now anyway — and the employee would take home roughly the same pay."

"Chaka," came in Wilson, "what are you really saying? Are you saying that the employees' net pay would be converted to gross, and that the employer would pay a type of payroll tax? Because if that is what you mean, then I think that would be an enormous change. The administrative problems alone would be gigantic."

"They wouldn't be as bad as they are at present. My friend, Jackson Dube, works in the pay office of a big company, and he told me that with this new SITE tax, their life is a nightmare, especially at the end of the tax year. But look at it this way: the cost to the employer would be the same; the employees would take home the same pay, and the taxman would get the same money. But yes, Wilson, in another sense, you are right: there would be a big psychological difference for the workers. It is very discouraging when one earns more money through overtime, bonuses, commission, promotion and so on, only to have

24

ever-increasing chunks taken away by tax. Just think what it would do for productivity if what one earned was truly one's own to keep. And another benefit of this system is that the Receiver would get rid of millions of taxpayers, and employers would be rid of the huge administrative burden that PAYE entails."

Petrus, who had been listening silently but intently, interjected, "Hold it right there, I'll be back in a second." He dashed into Chaka's kitchen and came back with another six pack of beer. Chaka didn't think that his supply would last the discussion, let alone the rest of the day, so he asked Nonquase and Dabulamanzi to go to Mbezi's shebeen for some more.

"Right, Petrus, you wanted to say something."

"Yes, I like that system. The workers pay no taxes, but the capitalists do. That sounds like an ideal system to me; why is it only the first step in your tax reform?"

Chaka shook his head: "Because basic inequities would still exist. It would be easy for employers to cheat by understating their total wage bill on which the tax is based. At least under the present system there is some control because taxes deducted have to be reported to employees and there is a link between the tax and the so-called gross wage. Also, under our proposed system it would still be difficult to police the perks paid to employees — as it is at present — and employers would pay more and more in perks to avoid the payroll tax.

"And it must not be forgotten that take-home pay represents labour's share of added value. This is generally a constant at around 50%. In theory you cannot just increase wages without first increasing added value, but in practice this is being attempted all the time. What happens is that the wage increase merely finds its way into the price of things, causing another round of inflation and bringing the wage/added value ratio back to its correct balance. So this scheme is not to give employees an increase, but merely to cut out the administrative absurdities and to show that wages are not a valid target for taxation. Nevertheless, I do believe that this system would be an incentive for workers, and it's likely that there would be an overall increase in added value."

"I don't understand what you are talking about. What is added value? Do you mean profit?" asked Petrus.

"No. Added value is simply this: a carpenter buys some wood and some glue and screws and paint for say R15, makes a table, and sells it for R30. The added value is R15. Out of that R15 must come his assistant's wages, the interest on the money he borrowed to buy his equipment, and any taxes he must pay. What is left over is his profit. In other words, added value is gross sales less the cost of materials and expenses. Wages are not an expense because they are a factor of production and therefore are entitled to a share of added value along with the other two factors: land and capital."

At that moment there was a flurry of activity in the street and those in the

25

house looked out to see what was happening.

"Ah," said Chaka in a pleased tone of voice, "these are friends of mine."

A car pulled up in front of Chaka's house, and out climbed Robert Armitage, Solomon Kgamphe and Michael Barnes. Chaka went out to greet them.

"I'm surprised that the police allowed you into Soweto today. There has been some trouble. But welcome to my home. This is Petrus Mhlope, and this is Wilson Radebe. My other guests were sent to get some more beer, but I think they have been waylaid by the new band at Mbezi's shebeen. Anyway, I see that you three come well supplied, so we needn't worry about dying of thirst before Dabulamanzi and Nonquase get back. Come in."

Petrus was wary of the newcomers; he seldom came into contact with whites who were not police or some other authority.

"Why have you come to Soweto?" he asked.

"To see our friend Chaka," replied Robert. "We have some unfinished business to discuss. Some time ago we discussed taxation and other matters, and Chaka left saying that we must meet again to come up with some answers. Now Chaka isn't an easy man to contact, so we took a chance that he would be home today and in the mood to continue our discussion."

"Your timing is perfect," said Chaka. "I have in fact just finished telling my friends here of that visit to your house and we were starting to put together some ideas about how the tax system could be changed to free up the economy.

"We have discussed the idea of abolishing all taxes on salaries and wages, and turning that tax on to the employers who really pay the tax anyway. I have talked about that with you many times, so I don't think that we need to go over it again now."

Wilson came in at this point. "Chaka says that taxes could be abolished because the state could collect all its revenue through 'user charges'. I find it hard to believe, because the state will want to know that it is going to get the revenue it needs, and I can't see how it can be assured of this. Also, this new system must be politically acceptable."

"I don't see a political problem," said Robert. "The changes you have mentioned will largely remove taxation from the individual, and when that happens it becomes difficult to make a big political issue out of taxation."

"The real problem," said Chaka, "is the change over to the new system."

"I think," said Michael, "that the system of municipal rating, especially in the Transvaal, holds the key. The system of site value rating is in effect a system of user charges and not a system of taxation. For instance, what the municipality in Johannesburg is doing is charging landowners for using the infrastructure of the community, and this charge is based on the value the community puts on each piece of land. And this is the fairest way because it is based, fairly closely anyway, on the market value of the land."

Petrus sat listening intently to all this. Although he was in his early twenties, he was still trying to get his matric at a Soweto high school. He had become very involved in student politics and with the young comrades, and had spent many hours discussing politics with his friends. It was a brand new experience for him to be in the company of people such as these: two white men of the 'capitalist class', two black men who would be in the same category if they weren't black, and Chaka. Dabulamanzi had deserted him, and Petrus was beginning to think that Chaka had turned the tables on him. Still, the beer was good, and Dabulamanzi was right: Chaka and his friends did have a point of view that was different and worth listening to.

"Petrus, my friend," said Chaka, "you are very quiet. What do you make of all this?"

"I can see a few problems, but I'll wait and listen to what your friends say."

"Well, I know of one immediate problem," said Robert. "The user charge would be based on the value of the land, and to make up the revenue needed by the State, it would have to be considerably higher than the present municipal rates. Now as these charges went up, the market value of the land would decrease. This system is like the famous wara-wara bird that flies in ever-decreasing circles — eventually you have a charge of 100% on a land value of nil."

"You're partially right, Robert," replied Michael. "But you forget one thing: it is the community that gives land its value, so while this user charge may lessen the value to the landowner, it does not lessen it for the community."

"A very good point, Michael," interrupted Solly, "but this is the problem: if the market does not determine the value, who is going to determine the value to the community?"

"The market, Solly, the market," said Michael.

"I don't understand; if you destroy the market, how can the market determine land values?"

"If the user charge was high, there certainly would be little or no value in the land as between seller and buyer. But as we have said, the value of land is created by the community and that value will go up or down depending on how the community values the land. The posh suburb today may be a slum in twenty years time; the ordinary middle-class suburb may be gentrified, or 'Chelsea-fied', and be in big demand by yuppies and arty types. The question is, how do we determine that the user charge remains fair over the years? Surely the answer lies in creating a land rent market."

"Why a 'land rent market'? How does rent suddenly come into the picture?" asked Petrus, completely confused by the whole argument.

"The user charge, Petrus, must be based on the rent of the land, in exactly the same way that the selling price of land today is based on a number of years rental. We are dealing with fundamental principles here. When more than one

27

person wants to use a piece of land it immediately acquires a value, and the owner of that land can then rent that land to the highest bidder. Now a user charge may diminish the value of the land to the owner, but not to the community or to potential users of that land. Potential users will still be willing to pay to use the land. The big difference is that the payment for the use of the land will go to the community which created the value in the first place."

"Okay, Michael," said Petrus, "I am beginning to understand. But I still don't see how you are going to create this 'land rent market'."

"Neither do I," said Solly.

"Well, an example of how it could be done was proposed by a Frenchman, V. Precy, in the 1930s. He suggested that every three years, or every five years in the case of rural property, an auction should be held, the bids being what the bidder is prepared to pay for the annual user charge payable to the local authority. If a bidder other than the present owner is successful, he would then be obliged to buy the existing improvements from the present owner, or rent them from him."[1]

Chaka had been listening intently to the discussion.

"Michael, I can see many problems in this scheme. For a start, there doesn't seem too much security of tenure for the occupier. Every three years he is subjected to the ordeal of an auction, at the end of which he could be out of his house or business or farm."

"Monsieur Precy thought of that, Chaka. He proposed that the dice be loaded in favour of the present owner. New bidders would have to declare themselves before the auction, and put up security equivalent to one year's user charge at the present rate. They would also have to demonstrate that they have the means to buy the improvements on the land. Also, the present owner need only meet the highest bid, not better it, for him to retain his property. He could also appeal against the new charge if he felt that the bids were mischievous and out of line with charges for similar properties."

"What about residential property?" asked Robert. "When this system comes in, there will be a huge gap between the present site value rates and a user charge for the property which is based on the value of the land. It wouldn't be possible to close that gap immediately."

"I don't see a problem with that," replied Michael. "The rates from residential property represent a fairly small proportion of the income of municipalities with a reasonable commercial or industrial base, and the same will apply under a user charge system. In the case of smaller towns, and the townships as well, land values are fairly low now, and the user charge would also be low. Eventually, under the auction system, the user charge on residential properties may creep up. Perhaps it will be necessary to dispense with the three-year auction and have an auction only when the owner wants to sell. In other words, as soon as the owner has agreed to sell to someone, the local authority holds an 'auction' for the annual user charge. The same rules apply: bidders must declare themselves before the auction, must be able to provide security for one year's user charge, and must be able to show that they can buy the house — a bond in principle from a bank or building society would be sufficient. If the highest bidder is not the one to whom the seller first agreed to sell, then the first agreement falls away and the property goes to the highest bidder, who must of course pay the seller the price at which he had agreed to sell in the first place.''

"How would you change from the present system to the auction system?'' asked Solly. "You couldn't just change from one to the other overnight.''

"Certainly not,'' replied Michael. "The change would take several years, and each component of the present system would be replaced one by one by the site user charge. The way I see it, every piece of land in the country would be valued at its present market value, or something as close to that as possible. That exercise alone could take a year. Then a site user charge at a specific percentage would be levied on this value, and this would replace a particular tax, say the payroll tax Chaka told you about earlier. The following year another tax would be replaced by an additional percentage on the site user charge. And so on until all taxes had been abolished. While this is happening, of course, land market values will be coming down as Robert mentioned earlier. This process mustn't take too long or distortions in the land values will start to take place. I think the auction system will take over quite naturally; in other words, the user charge on a site will be a certain amount and people will be prepared to pay that or they won't. The percentage on the so-called land value will be almost immaterial.''

"I don't know,'' said Solly, "it seems a very complicated system to me.''

"Compared to what?'' replied Michael. "The present system? Even the Johannesburg system of site value rating, which is said to be the best and fairest of municipal rating, is quite complicated. Every three years a new valuation roll is produced and it takes an enormous amount of work by the city valuer and his staff and their giant computer. Even then the new valuations produce a number of objections. The auction system would do away with all this and let the market determine the annual user charge. You couldn't ask for anything fairer and simpler than that.''

"Maybe,'' replied Solly somewhat sceptically, "but I think in any case that the principles are more important than the procedures. There are probably dozens of other procedures that would be equally effective. For example, I agree that this three-year auction is totally impracticable. The only time an auction should be held is when an owner genuinely wants to sell his property, and that would include the sale of shares in a property-owning company. The local authority, on behalf of the central government, should constantly monitor the changes in user charges as they are bid at the auctions, and calculate the average charges for similar properties. Where any property's user charge is, say, 10% or more off the average, then the local authority should have the right to make a unilateral adjustment, up or down. And, of course, always subject to appeal by the owner. Although the local authority would be updating its user charges all the time, it would be easier for everyone if the new charges were payable from, say, the beginning of each year.''

"That's right, Solly," said Robert. "And as regards the local authorities' slice of the pie, they would have the right to levy a percentage on top of the annual user charge payable to the state. Obviously whenever anyone took part in a 'user charge' auction he would know what this percentage is in advance and take it into account in making his bid. Needless to say, if Bloemfontein made their levy 10%, and East London only 1%, Bloemfontein would chase a lot of people away; this would provide a natural disincentive to greed on the part of the local authorities.''

"You made a very good point a moment ago, Solly," said Chaka. "You are quite right about the principle being more important than the procedure. What we must remember is that we are not just trying to find another source of revenue for the state. This user charge, if it is correctly based on the value the community places on the land, is merely a charge by the community for something it has created: the difference in the value of one piece of land over another. Taxation, the way it is structured at present, is robbery because it takes what belongs to others — the value created by labour and the value created by capital — and leaves virtually untouched what is created by the community. This demotivates labour and chases away capital and leaves us with the economic problems we have these days.''

"As a matter of fact," said Petrus, "now that Solly and Robert put it like that, it seems to make a lot of sense. After all, the person who buys a property decides for himself what his contribution to the community will be, so he can't complain.''

"Yes," said Michael, "and it wouldn't take long before people had a good idea of relative user charges. The authorities would be obliged to publish all user charges and no doubt the financial and other newspapers would highlight changes and trends as they do with share prices on the stock exchange at present. But in principle the auction system is simply a means whereby the state would collect the natural rent — its natural source of revenue. Given that this system would lead to much greater prosperity, it is very unlikely that the state would need more.''

At this point the door opened and in came Dabulamanzi and Nonquase looking very pleased with themselves and holding aloft the beers they were sent to buy.

"If we were to rely on you two," chided Chaka, "we would have died of thirst some time ago. Luckily, my friends came just in time to rescue us, not only from dying of thirst, but also from running out of ideas. You missed a good conversation; you must get Petrus to tell you about it. You have in fact met these gentlemen, even if not in the flesh. This is Robert Armitage, my accountant friend, whom I was telling you about earlier this morning; this is Solly Kgamphe, a lecturer at your university, Dabulamanzi; and this is Michael Barnes, who works for the same bank as you, Wilson."

The men all shook hands in the accepted African fashion, which surprised Petrus. Perhaps whiteys were not all the bogeymen he thought they were.

"Chaka, we must be going," said Robert. "Thank you for your hospitality, but more than anything, thank you for the conversation. And you mustn't wait a whole year before your next visit."

5 THE UTILITY MAXIMISATION OF PIGEONS

The study of economics does not seem to require any specialised gifts of an unusually high order. Is it not, intellectually regarded, a very easy subject compared with the higher branches of philosophy or pure science? An easy subject, at which very few excel! The paradox finds its explanation, perhaps, in that the master-economist must possess a rare combination of gifts. He must be mathematician, historian, statesman, philosopher – in some degree. No part of man's nature or his institutions must lie entirely outside his regard.

John Maynard Keynes

It was one of those glorious winter mornings in June when the comrades had ordered everyone to stay away from work, and Chaka was basking in the sun outside his little Soweto shoebox when a battered old Chev drew up at the gate in a cloud of dust. Out jumped Petrus with two other men, whom Chaka recognised as Dr Phalane, a township intellectual the Press loved to quote whenever the Government announced one of its 'reforms', and Reckson, a friend of Dabulamanzi and Petrus.

"So this is Chaka, the man with all these wonderful ideas for doing away with tax and giving land and instant Utopia to the people!" said Dr Phalane.

"Oh no, Doctor," Chaka said, "it's just common sense. Anyway, we've little else to do these days but think about how good life might be when apartheid goes."

"Well, our friend Petrus here has explained it to me and it all sounds very interesting — but I just want to ask you why no one has ever thought of this wonderful idea before. Why isn't it being done anywhere else in the world? Has Man never lived in harmony with Natural Law before? Has collection of the Natural Rent or this site user charge system of yours ever been tried elsewhere and why do you think we in South Africa should be the first to experiment with these new ideas?"

"Hau, Doctor! It is good you came early in the morning because you have asked some big questions. But come in and sit down. Petrus, please fetch some beer from the kitchen for the doctor and Reckson.

"But I must tell you, Doctor, if you really want the answers you will have to help me find them because right now I honestly don't know."

"Ag, come on, Chaka man, don't waste our time, just get on with it," shouted Petrus from the kitchen.

"Well, for a start, Doctor, can you tell me why Man took so long to discover the wheel, or to realise that the Earth is a spinning ball that revolves around the Sun? Can you tell me why the whites have only just woken up to the fact that apartheid is a disaster? You see, many of the greatest discoveries of Man seem blindingly obvious to us now."

"Certainly, I could never understand how the whites could not see the folly of apartheid — but they didn't!"

"The other thing to realise, Doctor, is that these ideas are not mine. They have been stated many times before by people like Henry George in *Progress and Poverty*, Leon MacLaren in the *Nature of Society*, and Fred Harrison in *The Power In the Land*, and even Sir Winston Churchill in *The People's Rights*. So, Doctor, you are a clever man: you can read these books and tell the people whether what old Chaka says is true."

"Chaka, why has nobody ever heard of these people's ideas before?"

"Once again, Doctor, I can only guess, but there are a few things which can be said. First hear Count Leo Tolstoy on this."

Chaka went over to his bookcase and pulled out some papers. He searched through them until he found the passage he was looking for, and then read aloud:

"George's idea... changes the way of living of the people, to the advantage of the big majority - at present downtrodden and silent... this idea is expressed so convincingly and effectively and above all, so simply that it is impossible not to understand it. For this reason there is only one way to fight against it, to falsify it and to keep silent about it. Both are practised with such pains that it is difficult to induce people to read George's books attentively and to deepen his doctrine. In the whole world, among the majority of intellectuals the ideas of George continue to be misinterpreted, and the indifference towards them appears to grow."[1]

Chaka put down the papers and continued: "It is also interesting to note how recent a development income tax is. It was introduced in America less than 80 years ago, but the way people talk today you'd think it came out of the Ark with Noah! In time to come, people will see it as a barbarous relic long before they stop using our gold. It will be as much a source of wonderment to youngsters reading their history books as the Spanish Inquisition is now.

"Then you asked me whether Man has ever lived in harmony with Natural Law before. That too, Doctor, is a big question, but briefly, the answer is yes."

"Where, Chaka?"

"Right here in South Africa, Doctor. Around this very gold-rich Ridge of the White Waters our forefathers lived in harmony with Natural Law, as far as economics is concerned. So did our brothers elsewhere in South Africa, the Khoi-Khoi and the San. For they were never so barbarous as to allow one of their own people to enclose the veld and make them pay to hunt there. Every man had an equal..."

"Yes, yes, Chaka, of course I know about our people, but who else?"

"Well, there were many examples in pre-industrial times. Of course there were many other nomadic semi-pastoral communities similar to our people, such as the Red Indians and the people of the Asian Steppes. But if you want to know about one such nation which had a system for settled agriculture which prevented big land-barons, then read the Bible!"

"An indaba on economics is one thing, Chaka, but don't waste our time with religion, man!" chipped in Petrus.

"Just read Leviticus 25, Doctor! There you will read about the Great Jubilee, every 50 years, when every man had to return to his own land and to his own family. In between Jubilees land could be bought and sold, but only for the time left till the next Jubilee. So no one class could end up owning all the land!

"Even in the feudal system of Europe land was held from the King in return for service. The peasants held land from the local baron, who held it from the duke and so on, in return for service. The barons and dukes provided protection and in return the people supported them. In theory, at any rate, there was no such thing as unrestricted freehold title without a corresponding duty to the community.

"Gradually, of course, this degenerated into the absolute right of ownership which the Europeans have today. One of the ways in which this happened was, for example, through the land enclosure acts which were pushed through the English Parliament over hundreds of years. The crunch for the small English landholders, the yeomen of Old England, came with the Agricultural Revolution. Many of them lived in villages in which each man had a right to keep so many cattle and sheep on the common grazing land and to cultivate various strips of land around the village. Each strip would be left fallow one year and planted in the second and third years. It was all very balanced and just and the people were happy.

"But of course, it was no good for the new methods and tools discovered in the Agricultural Revolution of the eighteenth century. So the land was fenced in by the few, and the many were turned out. Later, they provided cheap labour for the new factories of the Industrial Revolution, in which women and children worked in far worse conditions than even our people are used to here. The British and others found outlets for these people in their colonies, while the Germans later sought more space or 'lebensraum' through war.

34

"So the point is, Doctor, some people did indeed live to some extent in justice and harmony with Natural Law before the new inventions which needed fewer people on the land and more in the factories, mines and trade. Enclosing the land for that purpose may well have been good. What certainly was not good was the failure of governments to collect the rising natural rent from those people who took the land."

"And what happened in the cities, Chaka?" asked Dr Phalane, who seemed to be a little less sceptical now.

"Exactly the same as in Johannesburg, Doctor! When the poor whites in the thirties and the blacks after the war came to our cities, land values rose dramatically. The same thing happened in Europe! Landowners in and around the cities benefited from the growth in population and production but the new arrivals from the countryside didn't, because governments failed to collect the rising natural rents there as well!"

"So what did the people do about it?"

"Well, Doctor, they protested and struggled until, in Western Europe, they achieved democracy. But that still didn't solve the problem."

"Why not?"

"In a nutshell, Doctor, because they listened to the socialists instead of to people like Henry George, Churchill and Tolstoy. They thought that if governments owned the land and ran the industries, mines, banks and so on, everything would be all right. In fact, only now, after a century of socialism, are they beginning to see what a hash governments make when they interfere in this way. Socialism did give some of the benefits of industrialisation to the people, but if governments had simply collected the natural rents in the first place, the need for redistributing wealth via socialism would never have arisen."

"Chaka, you are a funny old man! Why do you talk about Churchill as if he were a great intellectual benefactor? Surely he was nothing but a war-mongering capitalist — and an imperialist to boot!"

"Well, Doctor, quite apart from the fact that he helped save the world from the jackboot of Hitler and fascism, do you know that as a young Minister in Britain before the First World War, he was an admirer of Henry George and tried to implement his ideas?"

"Nonsense, Chaka! As a young man he came here with the British when they fought the Boers. And they did that for the gold, not to help us!"

"Yes Doctor, that is true, but let me read to you what Churchill said about land."

Chaka went back to his bookcase, pulled out *The People's Rights*, turned to a well-thumbed page, and read aloud:

"*It is quite true that the land monopoly is not the only monopoly which exists, but it is by far the greatest of monopolies – it is a perpetual monopoly, and it is the mother of all other forms of monopoly. It is quite true that unearned increments in land are not the only form of* unearned or undeserved profit which individuals are able to secure; but it is the principal form of unearned increment which is derived from processes which are not merely not beneficial, but which are positively detrimental to the general public. Land, which is a necessity of human existence, which is the original source of all wealth, which is strictly limited in extent, which is fixed in geographical position – land, I say, differs from all other forms of property in these primary and fundamental conditions. Nothing is more amusing than to watch the efforts of our monopolist opponents to prove that other forms of property and increment are exactly the same and are similar in all respects to the unearned increment in land. They talk to us of the increased profits of a doctor or a lawyer from the growth of population in the towns in which they live. They talk to us of the profits of a railway through a greater degree of wealth and activity in the districts through which it runs. They tell us of the profits which are derived from a rise in stocks and shares, and even of those which are sometimes derived from the sale of pictures and works of art, and they ask us, as if it were the only complaint, 'Ought not all these other forms to be taxed too?'

"But see how misleading and false all these analogies are. The windfalls which people with artistic gifts are able from time to time to derive from the sale of a picture – from a Vandyke or a Holbein – may here and there be very considerable. But pictures do not get in anybody's way. They do not lay a toll on anybody's labour; they do not affect any of the creative processes upon which the material well-being of millions depends; and if a rise in stocks and shares confers profits on the fortunate holders far beyond what they expected, or indeed, deserved, nevertheless, that profit has not been reaped by withholding from the community the land which it needs, but, on the contrary, apart from mere gambling, it has been reaped by applying industry with the capital without which it could not be carried on. If the railway makes greater profits, it is usually because it carries more goods and more passengers. If a doctor or a lawyer enjoys a better practice, it is because the doctor attends more patients and more exacting patients, and because the lawyer pleads more suits in the courts and more important suits. At every stage the doctor or the lawyer is giving service in return for his fees, and if the service is too poor or the fees are too high, other doctors and other lawyers can come freely into competition. There is constant service, there is constant competition; there is no monopoly, there is no injury to the public interest, there is no impediment to the general progress.

"Fancy comparing these healthy processes with the enrichment which comes to the landlord who happens to own a plot of land on the outskirts or at the centre of one of our great cities, who watches the busy population around him making the city larger, richer, more convenient, more famous every day, and all the while sits still and does nothing. Roads are made, streets are made, railway services are improved, electric light turns night into day, electric trams glide swiftly to and fro, water is brought from reservoirs a hundred miles off in the mountains – and all the while the landlord sits still. Every one of those improvements is effected by the labour and at the cost of other people. Many of the most important are effected at the cost of the municipality and of the ratepayers. To not one of those improvements does the land monopolist as a land monopolist contribute, and yet by every one of them the value of his land is sensibly enhanced. He renders no service to the community, he contributes nothing *to the general welfare; he contributes nothing even to the process from which his own enrichment is derived."*

"Well, I must admit, Chaka, that seems to make sense. Now tell me why, if Churchill's party was in power, the British don't have it now?"

As few South Africans understand the British and their politics now, let alone three-quarters of a century ago, Chaka couldn't really help Doctor Phalane. However, Chaka remembered someone telling him that the Liberal Party, to which Churchill belonged at the time, did introduce the principle in the 1909-10 Budget. Apparently it was very badly drafted and unworkable and even failed to introduce the simple principle of a straightforward rate on the actual value of land. So he said, "It seems, Doctor, that Churchill was sabotaged by the verkrampte bureaucrats just the same way the verligte Nats said P W Botha was with his reforms — such as they were." And then Chaka quoted from the foreword to Churchill's book from which he had just read.

"As it was, the great power and intellectual prowess of the Liberal Movement, which had commanded worldwide admiration for the breadth and nobility of its vision, was soon to be dissipated by war, internal feuding and the fear of bolshevism.

"Under the cruel heel of war and unemployment men came to value security more and independence less. The emphasis in social advance shifted to the massive provision of public benefits and the increasing intervention of the State in almost every area of human activity. The two World Wars and the great depression between them had to a great extent severed the line of liberal thought that had developed over the previous century."

Chaka then told Dr Phalane that the British Finance Act of 1931 introduced by Ramsay MacDonald's Government provided for a small land value tax based on a land valuation which was also to be available for local government rates. However, it was suspended before implementation and then repealed by the National Government which came to power soon afterwards. Dr Phalane, however, was not easily satisfied.

"Never mind the British, Chaka, didn't anyone else try it?"

"Yes of course! The Danes had a very successful experiment with the land tax which their government imposed from 1957 to 1960.[2] The Taiwanese, thanks to Sun Yat-Sen, who also read Henry George, benefited from these ideas, which were applied to land reform after the Nationalists crossed from Mainland China in the 1940s. The few feudal barons who owned the island at the time were bought out with government bonds and the people given land for an appropriate annual fee. Soon they exported food, the dollars from which were used by their businessmen to import machines for their factories, and since then they've never looked back!

"Even the Japanese, Doctor, have benefited to some extent from these ideas. After the Meiji Restoration in 1868 they had a land reform which helped them in the same way. In 1873 land surveys were begun to determine the amount and value of land on the basis of average yield in recent years, and a tax

37

in money of three per cent of the value was then set as the land tax. The same surveys introduced certificates of land ownership for farmers, who were also released from feudal controls. The establishment of private ownership, along with measures to promote new technology, fertilisers and seeds, soon produced a rise in recorded agricultural output. The land tax, supplemented by printed money, was the principal source of the government's income for several decades. However, by the end of the Second World War, the new landlords were living in the towns and taking two-thirds of the crops from their tenants. After paying for seed and fertiliser, these tenants were lucky if they got one-sixth of the crop to live on! But, as luck would have it, General Douglas MacArthur was an admirer of Henry George; he not only gave them a democratic constitution, but he also reversed the proportion so the tenants had two-thirds. Soon Japan was exporting rice instead of importing it!

"And then, Doctor, don't drop your beer, but right here in Johannesburg these ideas have been applied."

"Go on, Chaka, just now you'll be telling me the Boers are angels!"

"Not so, Doctor, but soon you'll be able to buy land in Johannesburg, and when you do, you'll have to pay the City Council site value rates whether you have a building on your land or not."

"Ag man, Chaka, I know that, but so what?"

"What we don't realise is that in Britain and America most cities levy rates or property taxes on the value of the buildings or, even worse, on the rental income of the property. So they penalise those who develop and use their land to the full and reward those who don't. Then they add rent control — and wonder why they get slums like Harlem in New York! In many cities of the West you can see vacant land near the city centres, or land with only a panelbeater's shop when it should have a skyscraper on it.

"So these cities lose out on revenue and encourage even the most blatant and wasteful forms of land speculation. Not so in Johannesburg. The panelbeater next to the Carlton Centre pays the same rates. Bare land pays the same rates as fully developed, according to its value. So, people develop their land! The builders just can't wait for the bulldozers to finish clearing the site because they are in such a hurry to get the new building up. I heard a story the other day that a builder had some of his materials carried off by mistake in the breaker's dump trucks because he put them on the site too early!

"It's not just the gold and the invigorating climate of the Reef that have made Johannesburg one of Africa's most dynamic cities. It rewards people who develop their land by not charging them a penny more in rates than those who don't. It's not just the sleepy climate at the coast that makes for slower development in places like Cape Town — they tax buildings and improvements! Imagine, Doctor, you build another room on your house for your mother and the City Council comes and says, that'll cost you R15 a month in extra rates!"

"You know what would happen if they tried that nonsense in Soweto!"

"Yes, Doctor! And you know, the interesting thing is that most people in America and Europe are so ignorant of site value rating that their City Treasurers don't believe it can be done. The Johannesburg Valuation Department happens to be way ahead of them in the accuracy and efficiency of its computerised valuation roll. In fact, their officials have been told when visiting America that it would be impossible to introduce this in some cities because the Mafia wouldn't like it!

"But even the people of Johannesburg don't know what a gem they have in their system. A few years ago their Council asked the Government to let them abolish site value rating and have sales tax instead. Fortunately someone realised that city revenues could be supplemented simply by making government departments pay normal city rates. This step would kill two birds with one stone because it would make the bureaucrats more cost-effective by showing everybody their true costs. In a rare moment of enlightenment the Government did this some years ago, and you know what?"

"No."

"The railway people suddenly discovered a few years later that this R50 million a year in rates was hurting, so they are now either selling or going to re-develop most of their vast land holdings in city centres throughout South Africa. So, hey presto, we've suddenly got 'new land' in all our cities!

"And then, of course, there are cases where governments, by luck or accident, give partial recognition to these principles without really understanding what they are doing. For example, public lands or off-shore gas and oil deposits are sometimes leased by governments on a tender or market-value-related basis. Before our gold bonanza began in 1972 the government used to give a 'subsidy' to the lowest grade or marginal mines. In fact, they were only repaying taxes — sales tax, customs and excise, the income tax paid by their employees — which these mines, being marginal and therefore yielding no rent, should never have paid in the first place. The wisdom of this course was shown when the bonanza began and the mines, which had been just as marginal as, say, the worst farming land, ceased being marginal and repaid the Government's 'generosity' many times over.

"Likewise, governments the world over attempt to counteract the disastrous effects of taxation on outlying marginal areas through subsidies and development grants and so on. However, whether it be Northern Ireland, Scotland, the North of England, the South of Italy or the Limpopo and other 'border' farms here, the subsidies succeed only to the extent that they eliminate the effects of taxation on marginal land. To make matters worse, subsidies sometimes increase land prices because wealthy people buy farms so as to offset their losses on them against income from elsewhere in order to reduce their

39

income tax. This makes it difficult for the young man who wants to be a farmer to start on his own. Since the subsidies are usually limited to new businesses they do not provide for all the other sites in the area. Bearing in mind the number of bureaucrats involved in giving out the subsidies, it is no wonder that they are at best cumbersome and costly, and at worst, ineffective and a temptation to corruption."

"Yes, Chaka, but surely the economists of the Western world would have cottoned on to these ideas of George and Churchill. What have they been doing?"

"Doctor, these things are difficult for us to understand. But if you look at economists today they seem to be very busy people. Some of them are employed by trade unions and universities and they are busy justifying higher taxes and socialistic measures to help the poorer classes, i.e. 'Labour'. Others work for employers to point out the need for low taxes to encourage capital investment to create more jobs. Still others busy themselves with computers trying to forecast what is going to happen to prices, wages and trade in general. So while some worry about the proper return to Labour, others about Capital and others about the future, none of them see land and its natural rent, even though failure to collect the natural rent harms both Labour and Capital.

"You know, Doctor, how people tell jokes about economists? But some of the economists themselves sense that there is something wrong with the approach to the subject nowadays. Look, for example, at what Robert Kuttner said in this article in *The Atlantic Monthly* in February 1985:

"The deductive method of practising economic science creates a professional ethic of studied myopia. Apprentice economists are relieved of the need to learn much about the complexities of human motivation, the messy universe of economic institutions, or the real dynamics of technological change. In economics, deduction drives out empiricism. Those who have real empirical curiosity and insight about the workings of banks, corporations, product technologies, trade unions, economic history, or individual behaviour are dismissed as casual empiricists, literary historians, or sociologists, and marginalized within the profession. In their place departments of economics are graduating a generation of idiot savants, brilliant at esoteric mathematics yet innocent of actual economic life."

Petrus laughed. "No wonder Dabulamanzi finds economics difficult!"

Chaka continued: "Later in the same article he says:

"Among the most astringent critics of the overmathematization of economics is one of the profession's most notable mathematicians, Wassily Leontief... Leontief tabulated recent articles in the American Economic Review. *In the period from March, 1977, to December, 1981, Leontief found, 54 per cent of AER articles were 'mathematical models without any data.' Another 22 per cent drew statistical inferences from data generated for some other purpose. Another 12 per cent used analysis with no data. Half of one per cent of the articles used direct empirical analysis of data generated by the author. Leontief says that a more recent tabulation finds the trend unabated. 'We found exactly one piece of empirical*

research, and it was about the utility maximization of pigeons!'

"So you see, Doctor, when I read that I think it's no wonder that ordinary folk don't understand what economists are saying."

"Yes, Chaka, it seems like they're only talking to themselves!"

"It's too bad, because many of these people are brilliant. If they could only come down to earth and see land and recognise rent, they could help the world polish off the problem of poverty before breakfast," said Chaka.

"That's about all the time we've got, Chaka. Maybe you should get the message across to them right away. Otherwise there's going to be a rare old bust-up down here, apartheid or no apartheid."

With that, the learned Doctor and his friends downed the last of Chaka's beer and left him in peace!

6 SIMPLE IS BEAUTIFUL

The principles that guide us in public and in private, as they are not of our devising, but moulded into the nature and essence of things, will endure with the sun and moon – long, very long after Whig and Tory, Stuart and Brunswick, and all such miserable baubles and playthings of the hour, are vanished from existence and from memory.

Edmund Burke

"Hey, Chaka man, where are you going? Just because you're on the box nowadays doesn't mean you can't greet people, you know!"

Many people were pulling his leg at the time about his namesake, the famous Zulu king, who was being portrayed in a television serial; Chaka recognised Reckson, who had invaded his house with Dr Phalane some weeks earlier.

"Home, my son," he said.

"Nonsense, old rascal, you're coming with me to Soweto Suzy's — this time the drinks are on us. Doctor's friends are there and want to hear more about your ideas."

When they got to the shebeen, sure enough, they were there and once again wasted no time on preliminaries. Before Chaka even had a glass in his hand the young man, Reckson, said, "Chaka, we've talked again about the things you said but we don't have time to read like you said we must. Just tell us more in plain language what it's all about. You obviously have a completely different approach to politics."

"Politics! I know nothing about that. It's far too complicated. Half the time I can never understand the reasons politicians give for their actions. Take apartheid, or the Nat's five-year plan. Or take anti-apartheid actions like sanctions, trade boycotts, disinvestment and school boycotts. Whether it's pro or anti-apartheid politicians talking, the things they say never seem to me to add up. There's only one thing in politics I pay any attention to, and that's the promises politicians make in order to get or stay in power."

"So what are all these things you're talking about? Economics?"

"Yes, Reckson."

"All right, Chaka. So it's economics to which you have a very different approach. Tell us, then, what economics is all about."

"Would you be happy, Reckson, if I said — the production and distribution of wealth?"

"No, of course not!"

"What would you say then, Reckson?"

"Well, of course you should add — by man from land!"

"Excellent, but why?"

"Me tell you? Don't you remember at your house we agreed that whenever men enclosed land the rent which arose from this should be taken by the community — and that this was a basic natural law which, if ignored, would result in poverty and strife?"

"Yes Reckson, but don't you think there might be other such laws?"

At this Reckson looked a little taken aback, but before he could answer, Wilson, the Dube bank manager, said, "Like the basic need for men to trust and believe in each other..."

"...and for bankers to decide how much!" they all chorused together with much laughter.

"Yes, and what about money, inflation, prices, booms, recessions, foreign exchange and trade and the proper role of the state?" Chaka said. "Don't you suppose that if there are natural and just laws governing access to land and credit there are also such laws governing these things too?"

"I don't see why not," said Reckson.

"And aren't all these laws about Man?"

"Yes."

"So can't we just say that economics is the natural law governing all aspects of the production and distribution of wealth by people when they live and trade with each other?"

"Sure."

"So, like other basic laws governing man, economics should be easy to understand for all?"

"Yes."

"I beg to differ," said Dabulamanzi. "Even if I had more time to study I'm sure I would not find it any easier."

"Thank you, Dabulamanzi," said Chaka, "because that may just prove the point. But perhaps if we talk about some basic economic phenomena from the point of view of natural law we can get at least some idea of the simplicity which in fact underlies the subject. I mean maybe we could look to see if there are other economic duties in addition to paying rent. Then we could look at the complications which arise if the rent is not collected; the effects of tax, bad attitudes to work, and so on. Then, although I don't think we have time, we could look at cycles, free trade and the natural role of government in the affairs of mankind."

"All right, Chaka," said Dabulamanzi, "let's go for it."

"We've agreed that so long as a man pays the rent he keeps his land and all his property on it. But what if he spoils it, either by overgrazing or by some other bad farming practice? Should we allow that?"

"No!" they said.

"And what if he emits pollution or uses his land in such a way as to be a nuisance to his neighbours — can we allow that?" asked Chaka.

"No."

"What about the loafers and tsotsis who could work but don't? Must we support them?"

"Of course not."

"Why not?"

"Well, I suppose it would be like paying them to rob us."

"So to sum up, we can say that there are some fundamental economic laws or duties governing the individual and they are simply, to support himself and his family if he is able, to keep the land in good condition, to pay the full rent, and not to disturb the quiet enjoyment by another of his land."

"Yes," said Reckson, "but what about the Government in all this — what must it do, apart from seeing that individuals carry out these duties?"

"Good question," Chaka said. "But first, do you agree that if the state is to enforce these duties of the individual it must look after those genuinely incapable of looking after themselves, ensure that individuals keep their land in good condition, look after vacant or public land, collect the full rent, and ensure that individuals are not disturbed in the quiet enjoyment of their land?"

They all nodded in agreement.

"Bravo," said Chaka. "Now, there are no doubt other laws governing economics, but these are the basic laws for the individual and the state. Most modern problems such as poverty, unemployment, inflation, break-up of family life, pollution, wild booms and depressions can be traced to ignoring these simple basic duties."

"Not so fast, old man!" said Reckson. "I was looking forward to hearing you try to show us the other so-called natural laws of economics and proving they weren't just a few more of these airy-fairy duties. But we can't let you get away with sweeping statements like that! Tell us, Chaka, what on earth inflation has to do with these duties of yours!"

"Hau, Reckson! I suppose then you'll want to know about depressions. Soweto Suzy hasn't got enough beer to last while we talk about all these things!"

"Oppas, Chaka!" boomed Soweto Suzy herself, arriving at the table just then with a tray full of cold beer. "We never close — even for police raids — and the liquor here has never run out before the talk! So drink your draught like a man and answer the questions!"

There was clearly no escaping the thirst of these people — for beer or talk — so Chaka swallowed long and hard and continued.

"I take it you agree that all wealth is produced by the application of labour and capital on land? Good. Well, the returns to labour are wages, to capital profits and to land, rent, and the total of those three is called added value. Given the equal application of labour and capital, the only reason for differences in added value on various sites is the quality of the site in relation to sites used by similar businesses.

"Now, Reckson, tell me, if the community collects the natural rent, what will it collect from the most marginal site in use?"

"Nothing," said Reckson, "because, by definition, it will have no advantage over other land and therefore the man who works it is entitled to all he produces on it."

"Excellent, my friend!" said Chaka. "So what will a man think about first before deciding to work for someone else?"

"Well, obviously he won't work for anyone else if he can make more by working for himself on land which is available free of rent," said Reckson.

"Quite so, Reckson," said Chaka. "So what will determine the general level of wages throughout the country?"

"Put simply, Chaka, it will have to equal what can be produced on the least productive, or marginal, land."

"That's right, Reckson. And because the community is collecting the natural rent on land there will generally be land available at the margin on which people can work for little or no rent — free land, in fact."

"Yes, but why don't you forget about this Utopia of yours and show us what is happening now, where the state collects taxes instead of rent?"

"I shall try, Reckson," said Chaka. "You can make my job easier by telling me what choices you have regarding work under our present system."

"Well, for a start there's no land available on which I can go and work without paying rent and taxes."

"Right," said Chaka.

"So either I work for someone else or I beg."

"Good. So now, Reckson, can you tell me what governs the general level of wages?"

"Well, we either agree with our boss or the trade union negotiates for us. If times are good and I know I can get more somewhere else, I ask him to raise my wages. If times are bad, I won't even bother to ask because I know he's looking for an excuse to sack people."

45

"What would you do if times were bad and your boss said he was going to halve your wages?"

"Frankly, I would be so insulted I would tell him to go jump, and I would cadge off my friends and family instead."

"The bosses are lucky we are so ready to help each other," said Chaka. "In Europe people out of work get big handouts which cost their governments a fortune. But, getting back to the point, can we not simply say that, when land is no longer free, the level of wages drops to the least men will accept? This level, in turn, is governed by the general level of trade so that when the economy is booming it moves up and vice versa."

"Maybe," said Reckson, "but why should simply having a tax system like the one today instead of collecting the natural rent, cause the level of wages to drop? Businesses operating on marginal sites will pay hardly any company tax because they are not making much profit, and to be honest, I don't see much difference between a charge on the natural rent, and company tax."

"That's a good point, Reckson," replied Chaka, "but you've forgotten all the other taxes which people on marginal sites have to pay, and which have very little to do with their profitability or ability to pay. Like GST, petrol taxes import duties, and PAYE on wages and salaries. A good example is the marginal gold mines which are threatened with closure when the gold price goes down. The government often subsidises these mines, but what is the subsidy? Only a return of the GST, PAYE and so on that the mine has been paying all along? Without these taxes, the marginal mines would probably be profitable at quite a low gold price.

"And like a drop in the gold price affects marginal mines, a downturn in the economy will affect all businesses operating on marginal sites. But the indirect taxes don't stop just because they're less profitable than before. So marginal sites start going out of production, unemployment goes up, and with increased competition for jobs, wages must come down.

"Only when wages have reached a level where marginal sites could pay taxes and still achieve an acceptable return on capital, would they come back into production. But when things pick up, profits and the landlord's claim increase first. Then, especially if people have the power to form trade unions, wages begin to rise. The entrepreneurs, who also have to meet landlord's rising claims, put prices up and so on.

"What is really happening is that everybody else is trying to restore their claim on production, or in other words their slice of the pie. These have been made smaller both by the landlord's claim — for which of course he has made no equivalent input — and by the fact that taxation is charged indiscriminately on businesses with little or no taxable capacity, i.e. the marginal sites. This forces them out of business. It is no wonder therefore that claims on production tend to increase faster than production. This results in inflation. Don't forget that when conditions improve there are still enormous pressures on governments. They must increase their share in order to mitigate the effects of poverty and injustice which result from their failure to collect the natural rent and their taxation instead of production.

"Eventually, after all spare resources of labour and capital are in use, property rentals and inflation get out of hand and business conditions decline. At this point governments have a choice. In the past they very often carried on spending and allowing the money supply to increase in the hope that they could avoid recession and unemployment. But that was seen to lead to runaway inflation, which reached 25% in Britain in 1980 — and it still didn't stop unemployment and recession. In fact, it made it worse. So nowadays many governments choose instead not to allow money supply to increase faster than production. This may take place with a cut-back in state spending, or increased interest rates resulting in business failures and unemployment. This reduction in the claims of wages and profits eventually brings about a reduction in property rentals including, of course, the landlord's claim.

"At the same time, if the governments have been successful in curbing their spending to some extent, inflation falls and they can point to the success of their policy, for now there is plenty of excess capacity in the economy and they can allow interest rates to decline in order to encourage economic recovery. This was the pattern in the early Eighties in North America and Western Europe. Of course, this success was bought at a record rate of unemployment and bankruptcies. Our authorities hoped for similar success for their anti-inflation policies — as well they might in light of unemployment here. However, the flight of capital, coupled with rampant government spending and price increases imposed by public sector corporations, denied them success as regards inflation. Economic recovery was way below our needs and all they achieved was a surplus on the balance of payments.

"Yet, you see, the basic thought is the same. In the topsy-turvy world of taxation of production, inflation is unavoidable in recovery just as unemployment is unavoidable in anti-inflation-induced recessions.

"So when the economy is at full stretch, a period of unemployment of labour and capital becomes necessary, not just to reduce the stranglehold of rising wages on profits but, more importantly, to reverse the runaway landlord's claim. So, every time the economy is running smoothly it soon has to shoot itself in the foot to prevent itself from falling over. How's that for a Hobson's choice?

"The real thief in the night, of course, is taxation at the margin of production. Now, because we don't see the culprit we all adopt a beggar-my-neighbour approach. The people feel they're being cheated by the bosses, the businessmen know they're being hammered by taxes and hamstrung by government interference, and the governments — under enormous pressure to 'do something' about it — only make matters worse because they, too, don't know what's going on. And sure enough, this leads to the breaking of another natural law."

"I suppose," said Reckson, "you're going to say we should all go meekly back to our jobs and stop complaining!"

"Not exactly, Reckson. Yet the natural law is indeed that man must work — not just for what he gets, but for what he gives. The satisfaction of knowing that he is doing something useful, using his talents to the full, is what makes all the difference between drudgery and happiness. That is why the economist's measures of economic prosperity are so inadequate — because they have no way of measuring people's fulfillment and delight in their work — or the lack of it! Gross national product growth per person each year minus two per cent or plus five per cent tells you nothing about this.

"No doubt each of us knows a few people who are lucky enough to really enjoy their work. On the other hand, when people feel they're being exploited they no longer enjoy what they're doing. They hold back, work to rule, join trade unions and only get satisfaction out of securing the maximum money for the minimum work. Now my question to you is this. Despite what the so-called radicals say, the apartheid laws are going out of the window slowly, grudgingly, but they are going. Job reservation, prohibition of black membership of trade unions, Mixed Marriages Act, influx control and so on will be followed by the Group Areas Act and the Population Registration Act — we all know this. So, when they finally go, do you think this feeling of being exploited will change?"

"Well, Chaka, some of us feel that socialism is the answer."

"Like Zambia and Tanzania?" retorted Chaka. "Perhaps I should put my question about exploitation like this — what about our black brothers in America? What about the working classes and the poor in America and Europe, where there is no apartheid? Do they have this joy, this fulfillment in their work? Or do they all have chips on their shoulders? Do they feel they are being taken for a ride? Something is wrong and they don't know what."

"Well, Chaka old man, they must speak for themselves but I suppose from the little we know we must say they seem to feel the dice are loaded against them."

"Aikona, Reckson!" said Dabulamanzi, the student leader at Wits. "You're letting him off the hook too early." Turning to Chaka he said fiercely, "Are you telling me that under your natural law there would be no trade cycles and that everything would go swimmingly forever?"

"I should have let you do all the talking because I know that in between your important duties as Campus Chairman at Wits, you study economics there."

And, as the student leader looked as though he was going to follow up with another bombshell, Chaka hastily asked, "You were here when we agreed that

48

economics was about Man and that, just as there are cycles throughout animal and plant life and other aspects of nature ..."

"Yes, yes," he said impatiently.

"Well then, is it unreasonable to suppose that cycles exist in the sphere of economics?"

"I'm asking you the question," he growled.

"Quite so," said Chaka meekly. "But first tell me if I'm right in saying that there are cycles in all aspects of human affairs. Nations rise and fall as do civilisations, cultures, religions and companies; the life of every human being, if it is not cut short, consists of a time of growth, followed by activity and then rest; a man's career span consists of learning, running hard, then directing; women have very obvious cycles in their lives; every day has its cycle of preparation, activity and rest, is that not so?"

"Yes, of course," said Dabulamanzi.

"Well then, since we have agreed economics is very much a human affair, cycles will be present."

"Okay, but what's the point, if it's just going to lead to an excess of greed and speculation followed by fear and unemployment? That doesn't seem natural to me," he said peevishly.

"That's a very interesting point, Dabulamanzi. Tell me, why is it unnatural and foolish to jump off a cliff?"

"To use your language, Chaka, it is unnatural because Man is naturally endowed with enough reason to realise what will happen if he ignores a basic law of nature — in this case, that of gravity."

"Exactly, so if he decides to ignore the law and jump, too bad, the law still works and his bones are broken. Now, when individuals and governments ignore a fundamental principle of economic justice such as that rent must be paid by the individual and collected by the State, the law still works. Whatever progress is made will be dogged by injustices in the form of poverty, unemployment, inflation, bad attitudes to work and so on.

"But that's not all. This injustice turns the natural economic cycle of growth, activity and rest into an orgy of speculation and greed followed by a slump into depression and fear. Now, just as in nature winter is a time when the dead wood is pruned and the seed germinates, so the economy needs a time when the old can be put aside and the new prepared. Spring follows winter naturally, and so too the new businesses and creative ideas blossom forth into a blaze of glorious and happy activity. When they've been established their fruits can be enjoyed and this summer, or autumn if you like, is naturally a more restful time.

"Again, as is the case elsewhere in nature, there are cycles within cycles in economic activity. So we have the short-term trade cycle and the long-term.

"There is some evidence from the past that the short-term cycle was seven years. Joseph's cycle of seven fat years and seven lean years in Egypt might have had something to do with this. More recently the short-term cycle seems to have been running at around four to five years. This may have something to do with the ruling parties in government planning everything so as to be in a boom period at election time.

"The long-term cycle seems to be in the region of 50 to 55 years. Again, the Biblical concept of the 50-year Jubilee described in Leviticus 25 was no doubt connected with this. You see, the long-term cycle is really required for the blossoming of the major new technologies which have already been discovered and tried out in the previous cycle. Right now the world is beginning to enjoy the benefits of the age of electronics, the groundwork for which was laid in previous decades. The previous cycle which ended with the oil boom was clearly based on the application of technologies using cheap oil. Before that, in the second half of the nineteenth century, the world benefited from the use of steam on railways and ships, the groundwork for this having been laid in the first half of that century. No doubt, after several false starts in the second half of the twentieth century, the world will benefit at last from the safe application of nuclear power.

"Obviously there are many other examples. A nation which ignores these cycles does so at its peril, as did America and and Europe when they tried to prop up outdated steel and coal industries only to wake up and find they were sitting with the dead wood while the Japanese were decades ahead with the new."

At this point one of the party who had dozed off began to snore loudly and even Dabulamanzi exchanged chuckles with Chaka, who began to think his ordeal was over. However, just then some more students joined them and Dabulamanzi felt compelled to go on the attack again.

"Right, now then Chaka, what's so natural about allowing cheap imports from abroad like these Taiwanese and Zimbabwean clothes which cost so many of our people their jobs?"

"The need for free trade is rooted both in the need for man to work — remember, we said by giving of his best to others — and in his gregariousness."

"His what?"

"Well, man naturally seems to benefit from interaction with his fellows — whether it is sportsmen competing overseas, musicians playing abroad or visiting professors giving guest lectures. For the same reason men congregate together in cities — for it is here that the fruits of the earth may be processed by manufacture to suit our needs and more specialised services become available. But these cities need to exchange their goods and services with others, and likewise nations with nations. More trade means more wealth. So free trade world-wide simply means that men everywhere can benefit from the diverse gifts of nature and the skills of men over the entire Earth, provided they can give something useful in exchange.

"The only trouble is that with the whole world for a market some countries or companies may play tricks to crush competitors and grab it all for themselves. The Americans, for example, accused the Japanese colour TV manufacturers of hatching a plot with the Japanese authorities. This was to sell at high mark-ups in Japan while they used the notorious Japanese non-tariff barriers against imports to stop the Americans from selling their colour TVs in Japan, while they sold Japanese colour TVs at below cost in America. Having wiped out their American competitors, they not only had dominance of the U.S. market but also of the world market — and of course then they didn't sell below cost! This, if it was true, would have been a particularly nasty example of dumping.

"Now this is where governments can do something useful. They can see that games like these aren't played to the detriment of our people, but if the Taiwanese and Zimbabweans can sell us clothes at less than our own factories can, and they are not dumping — that should be a pleasure! Our own resources of labour and capital which couldn't compete would then be free to concentrate on something else where we have a natural advantage."

"But Chaka, we can't hope to compete with Japanese and Europeans — their own markets are so vast, their technology so far ahead."

"I won't pretend it will be easy. But try looking beyond apartheid to when we're accepted in the world again. Africa is our hinterland, for a start. Foreign capital and know-how will return. Our people can and must be educated better. We can process more of our natural wealth. Some of you youngsters here could be goldsmiths and jewellers. Why is it the Italians make more money by turning our gold into necklaces than we make by digging it? But these glimpses of a golden future depend on freedom — economic freedom. Our people must be free to produce what they want, where they want and with whom they want — without never-ending interference from a meddlesome bureaucracy — black or white. Even under apartheid black entrepreneurs have arisen — look at the taxi drivers, the panelbeaters, the shops, hairdressers, furniture-makers and so on. Imagine how much better off they would be without the restrictions of apartheid or any other heavy-handed state system."

"But Chaka, the Afrikaners lifted themselves up by control of the Government — shouldn't we blacks do the same?"

"Clearly, if blacks controlled the government they could do more to mitigate the effects of the poverty which results from an unjust system. But the cause of this poverty is not just apartheid — and so long as a black or any other government fails to address the root cause we shall be no better off."

"So what then is the role of government in this natural law of yours?"

"Government must govern and leave producers to produce. But to understand this seemingly glib answer to your question we need to see that there

51

is a natural and simple structure to the organisation of mankind. Thus government is at a higher level than the producers of goods and services — or what we might call the economic organism."

"Right at the bottom of this structure, or hierarchy, are those who wrest the raw materials we need from the surface of the earth. They are the farmers, miners, fishermen, timbermen, oil men and so on. They tend to live in simple village-type communities and a feature of their work is hard physical labour, even with the aid of modern technology.

"The next level is that of the larger towns or regional and industrial centres servicing these communities. In agricultural areas they would be market towns and in mining areas they might provide engineering and other back-up services or processing of the raw materials from the mines. Typically, higher levels of skill, even craftsmanship, would be present.

"At the third level of the structure we find the centres of trade, industry and finance from which most of the direction of the economic organism takes place. There is much more that can be said about these three levels but, briefly, together they constitute the economic organism which, when allowed to function naturally, will cater admirably for man's material needs.

"To meet man's higher needs there is another distinct level, the level of government in the broader sense. This fourth level includes not only the lawmakers, those who carry out the laws and the courts, but also the churches and universities. In the older nations these functions are often located in capital cities.

"In order to work properly, this level needs to be connected with yet higher levels which are said to exist in the natural organisation of mankind.

"However, these do not concern us now, so before anyone asks me about them, do you agree that the most successful organisations, whether they be schools, businesses or political parties, are those whose members carry out their own jobs without interfering with those of others?"

"Of course, Chaka."

"So is there any reason why the organisations of mankind should be any different?"

"Clearly not."

"And while it may be difficult for us to recognise the higher levels, is it not true that the first four levels of mankind exist plainly for all to see?"

"Of course."

"Then governments should govern and not try to dig coal, run factories, banks and shops etc?"

"Obviously, Chaka, your idea means a big reduction not only in the role Government plays now, but also in the role as seen by many for the people's government of the future. Coming back to my question, what exactly do you think Government should do?"

"Sound defence, foreign relations, the administration of justice and the maintenance of civil liberties are themselves vital for prosperity. But in the economic sphere the role of government need go no further than the four simple duties we mentioned earlier, i.e. to ensure that individuals' and vacant land are kept in good condition; to collect the natural rent; to see that people are not disturbed in the quiet enjoyment of their property; and to look after those genuinely incapable of doing so themselves."

"Looks as if the bureaucrats will have even less to do than they have now, Chaka! You won't be popular with much fewer jobs to hand out!"

"Yes, but do you think anyone would mind if they knew how much more easily they could get new jobs or set up their own businesses? Take the question of keeping the land in good condition. Here alone is a massive task which has been neglected in favour of ideology. Vast areas have been ruined either through overgrazing or cultivation of non-arable land. Land-use and restoration, maintenance of ecological balance and prevention of pollution all fall within this simple duty.

"In the prosperous society we envisage, when government collects the natural rent instead of taxation, those genuinely incapable of looking after themselves will be far fewer, since the basic cause of poverty will have been eliminated. In a really prosperous society with diverse cultures, it is not too far-fetched to imagine that people might prefer to pay for, and choose, their own education and health from a variety of private sources. Either way, the country would be able to afford the type of education needed to equip it for competition in world trade.

"So you see, friends, all I am saying is that the idea of paying rent instead of tax is not just a one-off panacea from Chaka's tired old brain. It is a fundamental principle of natural law, a little of which I have spoken of tonight. To sum up, it is one of four simple economic duties which apply, as different sides of the same coin, to individuals and government alike. If observed, they allow the three levels of the economic organisation of Man to function naturally without interference from government, which is then freed to concentrate on its role at the fourth level of this organisation. Then we spoke of some other aspects of natural law such as the need for Man to find fulfillment in work through realisation of his talents. Cycles and free trade are also natural phenomena which, properly understood, allow Man to develop and prosper. When one moves towards natural law, things become simpler and easier. The further away one goes, the more complicated and harder they get. And I'm sure I don't have to ask you which you prefer — simplicity and prosperity, or complexity and poverty?"

53

7   THE THUNDERING BANKHERD

Chaka stood patiently in a long line in Commissioner Street waiting for a mini-bus to take him home to Soweto. As he waited, he pondered the new turn of events. The ideas he had been propounding were not new: he had spoken of them often over the years. But whites had generally regarded them as socialist nonsense, while blacks had dismissed them as a defence of capitalism. Nobody had been interested. Now this seemed to be changing. It was as though people, realising that apartheid was at last on the way out, wanted to think about what should take its place.

His reverie was ended by a clap on the shoulder and a voice proclaiming, "So you don't look the worse for wear after that session at Suzy's last night, mdala. I'm glad I didn't have to talk and drink like that!"

"Years of practice," said Chaka, turning and smiling as he recognised Alfred Nkosi. Then, as they crammed into the little bus, Alfred said, "I was interested the way everybody laughed at what that bank manager said. Please tell me why."

Chaka laughed and told how he had been with Wilson and his friends when they asked what he thought about the nationalisation of banks as stipulated in the Freedom Charter. So Chaka had asked Wilson, "Would you rather run your own bank or have the politicians decide what loans you must make?"

"Of course I'd rather make the loans myself," said Wilson, whereupon his friends laughed and said he was just another capitalist who wanted to exploit the people.

"Give him a chance to explain why," said Chaka turning to Wilson.

"Well, Chaka, I know the people here. I know who is reliable and who can be trusted. I know when a man is going to be a successful panelbeater, builder or hairdresser or run a proper car repair shop and so on. If the politicians or 'comrades' run the show, I'll have to lend to their friends and then get sacked when my bank loses money."

"Well, why can't you make these loans now?" asked Chaka.

"Chaka, you must know the answer to that as well as I do. There used to be a million apartheid and other regulations which made it very difficult for the ordinary person in Soweto to start his own business. Many of these have gone, or are going, but it is still difficult for our people to get off the ground. The other problem is that I'm not allowed to make loans without security, which the ordinary person here is unable to provide. If I don't make loans on First World principles, the same way my bank does in Johannesburg and Cape Town, my bosses will think I'm irresponsible and say it just proves blacks can't be trusted and will never learn what banking is all about. At the moment all I can do is make loans to the petrol stations and some of the shopkeepers in the township. I can't lend to the up-and-coming members of the informal business sector, the hawkers, builders, plumbers and so on.

"Then there is a whole Third World situation here which my bank doesn't even know about. Take the burial societies or the savings clubs, stokvels, for instance. Or the church groups which want to channel their savings to help their own members here in Soweto rather than see it lost in the big financial institutions in Johannesburg. Then there are the loan sharks, 'skoppe' and Mashonisas. Many of these home-grown forms of finance are rooted in our African culture, and I am sure there are many opportunities for banks to get in at the grass roots and help them develop."

"All right, Wilson," said Chaka, "you've shown the banks do not meet the people's needs. Is this why the 'Comrades' and the UDF and so on want the banks nationalised?"

"Of course," they chorused.

"But do we agree that Wilson may have a point when he said the nationalised 'People's Bank' may grant the wrong loans to the wrong people for the wrong reasons?"

"Yes," they said a little reluctantly.

"And if the nationalised 'People's Bank' had turned down Sophie Themba's application for a loan for a new shebeen, she wouldn't be able to go around the corner to try her luck with a competing bank?"

"No," they agreed.

"And surely we don't want yet another system based on bribery?"

"Of course not."

"Well then, if nationalising the banks is not going to solve the problem, should we not try to see what is wrong with the banks as they are? Would it not be easy then to see what kind of banks we must have to meet the people's needs?"

"Sure," said Wilson.

"To do this, we have to go back three or four hundred years to the origins of banking in Europe. Now, Wilson, I heard that you studied the history of money in your banking course, so tell us, what sort of people in, say, London do you suppose would have been seen as honest and reliable enough to begin this business?"

"Well, Chaka, at that stage they had no paper money and used gold and silver, and it was the goldsmiths, because people who wanted their gold turned into jewellery and ornaments would only use people they could trust not to snip bits off for themselves, and who had safe vaults in which to store it."

"Right, Wilson! So what was the next step?"

"The merchants, who simply wanted to keep their gold somewhere, would leave it with the goldsmiths. Then instead of taking all the gold out when they wanted to make a large payment, they would simply ask the goldsmith to keep the gold for the person they wanted to pay. This they could do in person or by way of a letter or note to the goldsmith, which was probably how cheques began. To make payments even easier, some of them no doubt began to ask the goldsmith to issue them with 'promises to pay bearer on demand' against the gold they held with him. Provided the goldsmith always produced the gold on demand, people would come to accept his notes as being 'as good as gold' and, like magic, you have paper money. They could simply hand these notes to the people they wished to pay. These people would in turn use the notes as money or deposit them with their own goldsmiths or bankers who, instead of going to collect the gold from the first goldsmith, would offset them against their notes held by them. Maybe from time to time they would deliver gold to settle the net difference."

"That's right, Wilson," said Chaka. "So the goldsmith would soon find that most of the gold just stayed in his vault while the paper notes changed hands instead. Now what would stop him issuing more notes than he had gold?"

"Being by now a wealthy man, whose livelihood depended on his reputation for the utmost good faith and prudence, he would have to be sure that what he was doing was honest and responsible."

"All right, Wilson, can you think of something that would make him issue more notes? I'm thinking, for example, that around about the time we are discussing, the Agricultural and Industrial Revolutions began with the discovery of new methods and machinery. Where did the money come from to make the new machines and set up the new factories?"

"Well, what happened, Chaka, was that the inventors were either gentleman farmers or were able to interest such people, who in turn went to our goldsmith-bankers, bubbling over with enthusiasm at the prospects of mass-producing textiles and so on with the new machinery. No doubt some of these bankers thought it would be a good thing for England to have these new industries. So they decided to issue some of their 'promises to pay (gold and silver)' notes, in excess of the gold held by them, to these would-be machinery makers and textile manufacturers. However, being cautious and prudent men,

I can see that they would not have made these loans without security."

"And what would that be, Wilson?" asked Chaka.

"Land, Chaka. They would have either taken bonds or trusted that these gentlemen would sell their estates to repay the loans if the ventures failed. So right from the start this bold new step of the bankers in promising to pay more gold than they held was backed by excellent security. They never really took the risks of financing industry themselves, and to this day they have continued to lend in effect to the wealthy, and not to the ordinary people. Hence, I suppose, the origin of the saying that 'the rich get richer and the poor get poorer.' Later on, to provide more permanent capital, the limited liability company was invented. By this means the growing number of would-be businessmen could raise funds by selling shares in the new ventures to the wealthy merchants and landowners. These ventures, if successful, would then be in a position to expand further by raising loans from the bankers based on the security of their stock."

"I see, Wilson," said Chaka. "So the ordinary people, for example those who were turned off the land by the Enclosure Acts, would not themselves be able to set up on their own using the new machines? Our 'prudent' bankers wouldn't have to take the risks of deciding which, if any, of these former yeomen or small farmers were reliable or skilful enough to be backed on their own? So they would have to work for a pittance for the others, or emigrate? Perhaps, Wilson, you could tell us how it was that these so-called prudent men in international banks in the 1970s came to lend such vast amounts to Latin American and African countries, which, as we all now know, they cannot repay?"

"Well, that's easy, Chaka. Once the banker's main criterion is security and he himself does not have to assess the viability of the particular purpose for which the funds will be used, this sort of thing can happen quite easily. So when the oil producers deposited their vast surpluses with the bankers in the heyday of the oil boom of the Seventies and early Eighties, the bankers thought that lending to governments would be a good idea. For in the developed countries lending to governments was traditionally regarded as almost risk-free, because they could always repay by taxing the wealthy and the industries of their countries. But many of these Third World governments spent the money on grandiose unproductive projects, and when the commodity boom, on which many of their economies were based, collapsed, they were in the soup."

"So what you're saying, Wilson, is that bankers were ready to lend these vast sums to Third World governments but not to the millions of small potential producers in the poorer countries and that it was therefore wasted?"

"That's right, Chaka."

"And you say this is due to the fact that bankers from the time of the Industrial and Agricultural Revolutions began to lend on security instead of simply granting credit for production?"

"Yes ... but what exactly do you mean by simply granting credit for production?"

"I don't know, Wilson. But perhaps you can help me. You said just now that the Freedom Charter wants to nationalise the banks because they do not meet the needs of ordinary people. What are these needs? Are you saying that the banks should be lending to us so we can buy yachts and caravans or speculate in land or on the Stock Exchange?"

"Of course not, Chaka! I already said that I know many of our brothers in Soweto who have been working in Johannesburg all their lives and who are quite capable of setting up on their own as electricians, plumbers, builders, garage-owners or makers of furniture, pottery, clothes and so on. Maybe academic institutions should also have a means of assessing these artisans and giving them certificates of competence. Most of them never went to school and may not even be able to write, but boy, see what they can produce! In any event, I believe we bankers should be helping people to become bigger producers, not bigger spenders."

"Even when they can't give you security, Wilson?"

Wilson hesitated now and it was clear his true banking instincts were doing battle with his training as a 'responsible and prudent' bank official. At last he said, "Why yes, that's right, Chaka. I believe it is the duty of bankers to help people get off the ground, and I believe I would be able to tell those who were going to make it from those who were going to blow it."

"So if Soweto already had enough builders or garages or shops you wouldn't lend to any newcomers?"

"Quite so, Chaka. I would only lend if I could clearly see a need for the production proposed by the would-be producer."

"Right, Wilson, but tell me, if all the bankers in South Africa started giving credit like this, wouldn't it drive up the demand for, and therefore the cost of, the capital goods required for these new businesses? And wouldn't that lead to inflation?"

"Not if the bankers were sure their budding entrepreneurs had got their sums right. So if at any time there were shortages of machinery and labour because of some crazy boom they would hold back until things calmed down. In other words, Chaka, when I talk about lending for production I mean viable, profitable production. And so long as this granting of credit is restricted to putting freely available supplies of labour and machinery to work it cannot, by definition, be inflationary. On the contrary, increased production of this kind would result in more goods and services being available and, by competing with existing supplies, they would help keep prices down."

"What about home loans, Wilson?" asked Kazamulu. "With the economy so quiet right now, all you bankers can think of is muscling in on the building societies' traditional terrain. Isn't that going to be inflationary and do you call that 'giving credit for production'? And would you do that on this wonderful do-gooder basis of yours — I mean, without taking security?"

"Okay, Kazamulu," said Wilson. "I know some fancy houses have been built in Diepkloof Extension lately. So let me say that I'm talking firstly about the need for ordinary people to have a decent home of their own instead of two families living in a dining room like we still have here. Once a man has his own home, his wife will see to it, if necessary, that he works so as not to lose it. Secondly, she will be able to see that he is properly refreshed and rested so that he can work much more efficiently than if he is crowded into a backyard without proper sleep or privacy. Thirdly, he now has somewhere to put all the fancy things people like nowadays, so he may well be motivated to work harder than ever before — either to get these things or to improve his house. All this means that investment in housing, like education, is a guarantee of a more able, energetic work force and therefore more goods and services for all. So credit for these purposes I certainly regard as good for production. Yet because it is not as direct as credit for a business, and because for the average man it is going to take half his working life to repay, I would most certainly still take a bond on the man's house."

"Bravo, Wilson," said Chaka triumphantly. "I knew all along that you knew what banking is really all about! Now tell me something else. What do you make of things like the Stock Exchange, the Small Business Development Corporation, the Industrial Development Corporation, venture capital companies and so on?"

Wilson, who by now was warming to his theme, said, "From what we have said before, Chaka, it is clear that all these things arose because with land enclosure, the early bankers didn't really have to use their imagination and truly fulfil their function. There is nothing wrong with all these organisations you mention. They have arisen naturally to fulfil the need every society has for people whose prime function it is to decide which ventures and which producers, however large or small, deserve credit or finance. In fact, the need for this is so great that even if the banks start lending more imaginatively and creatively, there will still be a place for them. But I have a vision of millions of small businesses getting off the ground. For this sort of pinpointed, small lending, the local bank manager is uniquely well placed. After all, as a banker he has always had the magical power of 'creating money' for this purpose."

"But Wilson, I thought bankers only lent out money that other people had deposited with them and weren't using," said Kazamulu.

"Don't you remember, Kazamulu," said Wilson, "that we said the early goldsmith bankers soon discovered they could issue far more of their 'promises to pay' gold on demand than they had on deposit with them? And as long as they could go on giving the gold on demand, and as long as their 'loans in excess' of their gold were for viable projects, there was nothing wrong with this. In fact, all the rigmarole of bank regulation, liquid asset ratios, control of money supply and so on, has arisen because there was not a clearcut recognition that bankers had not only the power, but also the duty to grant credit, that is, to provide the money for production. In the process of granting this credit, they in fact create money, which goes to show that money is the servant of credit, not the other way round. But at the end of the day the truth is that there is one simple safeguard above all others which will prevent inflation and misallocation of resources."

"And what's that, Wilson?" asked Kazamulu.

"It is that the bankers simply fulfil their function, which is to grant credit for production only. And I don't mean just some production, but all production which is economically viable. That way the nation's resources of labour and capital will never be either overstretched — which leads to inflation — or idle — which leads to unemployment. That means they don't lend to a great big fat corporation which is simply going to speculate in land or blow money on some pet project — even if it can offer good security. Nor do they lend to governments which are going to build palaces and empty motorways. And perhaps they need to be a little more restrained in all the weird and wonderful ways in which they tempt ordinary folk to spend as if there was no tomorrow."

"So would you abolish all the rules and regulations governing banks, Wilson?" asked Chaka.

"There is no great urgency," said Wilson. "After all, the system works and people have trust in the banks. But clearly the more people understand what banking is really all about, and the more responsible the banks become, the less need there would be for such a lot of mechanical, detailed supervision. This is happening worldwide to some extent, but the field could be opened up to more new banks. After all, it's not so long ago that banking in this country was a closed shop whose members were a cosy cartel, licensed to print money while pretending through elaborate form-filling and accounting conventions not to. What's more, they never even had to stop snoring!"

Chaka asked quietly, "Do you think this awareness of function would be enough to wean the banks from their 'secured advance only' lending of the past?"

"Well, I can tell you one thing straight away, Chaka," said Wilson. "If this user charge thing you were talking about is introduced, I can't see the banks ever financing pure land speculation again. For while land will be much cheaper for the producer to acquire, the holding costs would make it impossible for the speculator to withhold land from use. There would be no more fiascos like Glen Anil and Corlett Drive; do you remember what happened? Some banks were left holding thousands of hectares of vacant land outside our cities when those developers-cum-speculators went under in the Stock Market crash of '69.

"Furthermore, although all the established businesses would still own

60

millions of rands worth of improvements on their properties which could be mortgaged, they would have to pay the going user charge regardless of whether they used them efficiently and made big profits or not. This would force the banks to look more closely at the ongoing efficiency of such businesses and not just at their balance sheets and property values. This tendency would be enhanced due to growing competition in business, resulting from easier access to land for newcomers, as well as better access to credit along the lines we have discussed."

For a moment there was silence. Then Chaka said, "That's very interesting, Wilson. So in effect you are suggesting that if, instead of nationalising the banks, we abolished tax and the community collected the natural rent on land instead, the banks would quite naturally come back to giving credit for production. They would wake up from their two-hundred-year sleep in which they gave loans only on security without considering whether they were for real production or not. And that, instead of just one People's Bank, which might have to be bribed to provide finance, there could be more banks entering the fray. Kazamulu here might even be able to set up in competition with you!"

"That's right, mdala. The more banks the merrier. And instead of a small herd of large bankers thundering in a stampede to give bigger and bigger loans for more massive and wasteful projects, we would have more bankers, large and small, ready to unleash the productive potential of our people for whatever new projects, large or small, they were really capable of tackling.

"And while we are talking about new banks, Chaka, I saw an interesting programme on TV about the Poor Bank in Bangladesh. It was started by a Bangladesh man who went back to his country with an MBA and a PhD from an American university, and who had worked in banks in the USA. But when he arrived home he threw away his textbooks because he saw they were of no use in meeting the needs of his people, many of whom are even poorer than ours. Instead, he started this Poor Bank which lends only to the poor, and only for production.

"All the borrowers are members of a group of friends who meet once a month with the banker who looks after their group, to discuss their needs. One woman, with seven children, and with an annual income of $84, was lent money for a loom. When this TV programme was made three years later, she had fifteen people working for her, and was earning $3000 a year.

"Because the borrowers meet regularly with their group and the banker, they trust one another. As a result, they only take money for capital items they can use properly, and there are very few bad debts. I believe that our people, with their stokvels and burial societies, are suited to this type of banking. Come to think of it, this is the kind of banking I would really like to do.

"And make no mistake about it, this kind of approach applies just as much to the First World part of our economy and, for that matter, to First World economies worldwide. Instead of encouraging people to get head over heels into debt for consumer goods, they could be encouraging them to get into business on their own."

'Well, Wilson, that's fine. I'm going home now because you've shown me there's nothing I need tell you about banking and that there are people in Soweto who really understand what it's all about."

8   THE BOEROCRATS

In the long quietude of the eighteenth century the Boer race was formed. In the vast unmysterious, thirsty landscape of the interior lay the true centre of South African settlement. When the Trekboers entered it with their flocks and tented wagons, they left the current of European life and lost the economic habits of the nations from which they had sprung... Their tenacity could degenerate into obstinacy, their power of endurance into resistance to innovation, and their self-respect into suspicion of the foreigner and contempt for their inferiors. For want of formal education and sufficient pastors, they read their Bibles intensively, drawing from the Old Testament, which spoke the authentic language of their lives, a justification of themselves, of their beliefs and their habits.

C.W. De Kiewiet

"Hau, mdala!" exclaimed Alfred. "And didn't you want to be a banker after hearing all that?"

"Aikona, Alfred," chuckled Chaka. "I'd fall for every sob story and be conned by every township genius. But Wilson's different; he's got what it takes."

"Listen, old man, why don't you come with me tomorrow night? You know I'm with the SABC? Well, I'm going to a braaivleis in Melville with two of my colleagues, Koos Terblanche, who's also a cameraman, and Sakkie Hamman, a newsman."

To cut a long story short, Chaka found himself the next evening sitting in a walled garden in the Chelsea-type suburb with Wilson Radebe, Alfred Nkosi and his Afrikaner yuppie friends. Inevitably, after they had exhausted the relative merits of rugby Springboks and Kaiser Chiefs soccer stars, the attention of this Boer-Black saamtrek turned to politics. Chaka kept out of the discussion at first, but was drawn in when they started talking about 1948, the year when the Afrikaner Nationalist Party won control of the country. Chaka was the only one who could remember those days so Koos asked him what it was like before apartheid.

Chaka said, "Well, the Whites were so firmly in control that the '48 election seemed very remote and irrelevant to us. But I suppose, when you think of it, we didn't feel quite so out of it. After all, we had just thronged the streets of Johannesburg with the Whites to cheer 'our' King George, his beautiful Queen and the pretty Princesses. Some of us had served him up north with the white soldiers. And next to General Smuts, the most brilliant member of the Cabinet was another Afrikaner, Jannie Hofmeyr, who made many hopeful statements about the future place of Blacks in South Africa. Anyway, once the Nationalists were in power they lost no time in making it brutally clear where we stood. So I suppose you could say we underestimated them at first."

"That's right, Chaka," said Koos. "While Smuts was winning the war and strutting the statesman's stage overseas founding the United Nations and so on, the Broederbond was plotting to win the peace. The returning soldiers felt neglected and fed up with the armchair patriots who profited at home while they were up north. My father was one of them and he fell for the Nats and their new slogan of apartheid."

"Ja, Koos," said Sakkie. "But they didn't just take the old segregation and baasskap and call it apartheid. It was a whole new ideology, a kind of state religion, which the academics in the Broederbond hatched in the late Thirties and Forties. Your father and other voters didn't really know what apartheid was, but the Broederbond did! So I suppose you could say our volk was hijacked."

"Ja," said Koos. "And then they took me and the other little Afrikaners out of the English schools and dosed us with their propaganda. After that Smuts and his Sappe never stood a chance of getting back into power."

"Do you mean to say," said Alfred, "that you Afrikaners weren't always so besotted with apartheid and the thousands of laws and regulations that went with it?"

"I've never really thought about it," said Koos. "But even in its heyday the Nationalist Party never had a complete monopoly on Afrikanerdom."

"To answer Alfred's question more fully, maybe you should go back to the beginning," said Chaka.

"You mean the first Afrikaners? They were the burghers that Van Riebeeck freed in 1657 from the Dutch East India Company's service to produce the food for the Dutch fleets which his bureaucrats couldn't grow well enough. But the Company controls and corruption were too much for them so they trekked into the interior to be free."

"So Afrikanerdom started as a move away from bureaucracy and corruption, Koos?" asked Chaka.

"That's right. And when the British came, they tried to tighten up control. So in 1837 the Afrikaners went on the Great Trek out of the Cape Colony. To be sure there were other factors such as 'overcrowding' and the British attitude to the Blacks, but essentially they trekked for freedom as they saw it. And they were free! That is why the early Trekker republics were chaotic affairs — because every Boer wanted to be free from controls, you know, president on his own plaas."

"And are you free now, Koos?" asked Chaka.

"Hell no. We must be the most overregulated people on earth. Half of us are in offices sending out forms and the other half have to fill them in and send them back. Our businessmen waste hours and days applying for licences, permits and exemptions. Control boards tell our farmers how much they can produce and at what price. Our journalists are restricted by hundreds of laws that tell them what they can and can't say. P.W.Botha even came down on the head of the SABC when he didn't toe the party line slavishly enough! And do we have taxes!" he said ruefully. "In fact...

> Methinks I am a prophet new inspired
> This blessed veld, this earth, this realm, this Africa,
> This nurse, this teeming womb of free republicans,
> Feared by their breed and famous for their birth
> Renowned for their fight with Empire...
> Is now leased out... I die pronouncing it.
> Those Boere, that were wont to conquer others,
> Have made a shameful conquest of themselves!"

"Ag Koos man," said Sakkie, "you may be the Bard of Melville but you don't expect Chaka and Alfred and Wilson to swallow that! They are the ones who are oppressed!"

"Sakkie, you don't understand. None of us are really free. Even though the Nats now say that apartheid is 'outmoded' we are still all prisoners of that idea, and that includes our bureaucrats who administer the mess! And we don't seem to know where we're going. At least Verwoerd had a vision which most of us believed and were inspired by at the time."

"Well, Koos," said Alfred, "if, as Sakkie says, the Afrikaners were hijacked by apartheid, what vision did they have of themselves before 1948?"

Koos' face suddenly lit up. "You know, I was sent by the SABC a few years ago to a meeting in Pretoria addressed by Sir Laurens van der Post — that Afrikaner who lives in England who writes about the Bushmen and is a friend of Prince Charles. We didn't report it properly, but he was talking about this very thing. He said the Afrikaner in the early years of this century was different. He was the one who had a world vision, while the British were still jingoes captivated by Empire. Those Afrikaners were self-confident and proud of the fight they had put up against the British. Smuts, now regarded as a traitor by many of his people, was one such Afrikaner. But he was misunderstood. After all, he and the other bittereinders in the Boer commandos surrendered only when the British agreed to let them keep their language and promised not to extend the non-racial franchise of the Cape Colony to the Transvaal and

Orange Free State. Then, on top of it all, Smuts went and persuaded the British Prime Minister, Campbell-Bannerman, to restore self-government to the ex-Republics only a few years after the Boer War.

"In effect, therefore, he not only won back control of the ex-Republics for the Afrikaner, he extended this control over the whole of South Africa. Far from selling out the Afrikaner to the British, he saw the Empire as a vehicle whereby the Afrikaner and South Africa as a whole could become a fully-fledged member of a great family of nations. Van der Post went on to say that Afrikaners of this calibre didn't feel threatened by either the British or the blacks. Their poets, playwrights, philosophers, statesmen, soldiers, sportsmen, scientists and medical men could hold their own with the best in the world and make a great contribution to Africa. These Afrikaners simply didn't feel the need for 'protection' via racist legislation. And then, of course, there were the Cape Afrikaners who were very much part and parcel of the liberal tradition of the Colony."

"That's all very well, Koos," said Alfred, "but how does that help us now? You know in *Cry the Beloved Country* which Alan Paton wrote some forty years ago Msimangu said, 'I have one great fear in my heart, that one day when they turn to loving they will find that we are turned to hating.' Now your Church seems to be turning away from apartheid and your politicians talk of reform, but still the damage is far from undone. Do you think you Afrikaners will ever turn to loving? And if not, is it because you are afraid we have turned to hating?"

Koos shook his head slowly. "No, Alfred, we are not afraid. You can say what you like about us, but we are not afraid. In the end the Afrikaners will do what they think is right even if it is hard. But perhaps Van der Post gave us a clue. He said he was asked once by T.S. Eliot what the hardest words were to say in the English language. Eventually, after he had tried all the longest words he knew, Eliot said, 'The hardest words to say are: *I'm sorry.*' Nor is it easier to say in Afrikaans, but maybe that's what we've got to do before we can regain our full stature and discover our true role in Africa. Even if that apology is too late and not accepted, maybe we've just got to say it for our own good, to break with this misguided chapter of our past. Then we can look you in the eye and start afresh together. The Dutch Reformed Church has indeed apologised for its past justification of apartheid, but it still remains to be seen whether it speaks for all Afrikaners."

"You may be right, Koos," said Chaka. "I am sure the Afrikaner has a bigger destiny than to be a desk-bound bureaucrat or policeman lording it over us. And it's good if, as you say, he is brave. Because it won't be easy. Nevertheless, if he does what you say, I am sure the rest of the world will come at last to another view of the Afrikaner which will include the positive attributes which his fellow Africans, despite their differences, have known all along were there."

"You know, Chaka, you've just reminded me of something. Have you ever heard how Smuts managed to persuade the British to give the Boers back their freedom after the Boer War?"

"No, but it must have taken some doing because the British were at the peak of their power as a world empire and the Boers were well and truly beaten."

"Well, when he went to see Campbell-Bannerman to ask for responsible government for the ex-Boer Republics, he looked him in the eye and said, 'You can either have the Boers for your friends or your enemies. You choose!' So the British Prime Minister thought long and hard about it — and eventually he let them have it! And what a deal it was! Despite their natural affinity for the Germans, the Boers under Smuts for the most part stood side by side with the British through two World Wars to defend that freedom — just when the British really needed friends!

"Now, Chaka, what you are saying seems to me to be this: despite the Boers *not* having trusted their black countrymen with their freedom the way the British did them, and in so doing having turned many blacks into enemies, it may still not be too late to do so!"

"Kolskoot, Koos!" said Chaka. "That indeed is our message to you!"

9 FREE MEN

... whose service is perfect freedom.
Book of Common Prayer.

"The only reason I came here this evening was that I heard that you said the other day you thought the Afrikaners were not free," said Dabulamanzi to Koos Terblanche. "At first I thought that was too good to be true. Then I realised it was right because the people have served notice on you Afrikaners that you are no longer free to push us around."

As if to prove the Afrikaner courage of which they had spoken at the braaivleis in Melville, Koos and Sakkie Hamman had accepted a return invitation from their friend Alfred Nkosi to his home in Soweto. Those present on this occasion included Wilson Radebe the banker, his friend Kazamulu, Chaka, and Robert Armitage.

"Nor do we want to," said Koos. "We're sorry for what has been done in the past. All we seek now is a way in which we can give you your freedom without losing ours."

"So what's wrong with one man one vote? You will still be represented in Parliament, which is more than we blacks are now."

"Dabulamanzi, you know perfectly well what the Afrikaners say to that," said Robert Armitage, laughing. "But I would put it more bluntly. They don't want you people to do what the Nationalists did to the English in 1948; that is, exploit nationalism to get and stay in power, push the minority group out of the Civil Service and then govern purely for sectional advantage. And I must say, having watched members of one ethnic group rule that way for 40 years I can't say I like the idea of another group taking its turn. I mean, I think we'd like a system where we all have a say now and then."

"Well, that's too bad," said Dabulamanzi. "You missed your chance. And if the English were as downtrodden as you say, why didn't they and their Mother Britain fight? The answer? They and Britain were 'fat cats' benefiting from living with apartheid and trading with it. And quite frankly, why shouldn't blacks take over the Civil Service when they come to power? If the Afrikaner needed that kind of thing to get even with the English, then clearly we need it in order to catch up with the Afrikaner. And you watch, we won't be as harsh on them as they were on us. In any case, how can you expect the people — I mean us taxpayers —" he said this with a laugh, for the Wits student leader was an ardent socialist, "to support the one out of every two working Afrikaners who is employed by the public sector?"

"I don't blame you for feeling the way you do, Dabulamanzi," said Sakkie. "But the fact is, we Afrikaners are just not going to hand over to you so you can get your own back on us. Share power yes, surrender no!"

"And what's all this sharing of power about? You mean the minority have a veto so we all have to agree before anything is done? Man, we aren't going to buy that because the Whites will just use it to protect their privileges."

"Now wait a minute, people," said Alfred. "Chaka, before they come to blows, what do you think? And don't try to wriggle out of it again."

"There you go again," said Chaka, "always trying to drag me into politics which I know nothing about. You see, I understand how Dabulamanzi and Sakkie feel. They're both right in one way. And yet in another, they're both wrong."

"What do you mean, Chaka!" "Get off the fence, man!" they all exclaimed indignantly.

"Well, they are both right in that they seem to realise that removing apartheid alone will not put an end to poverty. But then they both assume that the only way for oppressed people to achieve equality is to grab control of the government and then dish out the goodies to themselves. Now, so long as you do not eliminate the cause of poverty, then that is so. The trouble is, as we have seen elsewhere in Africa, the only equality this achieves is the equality of misery and poverty, because usually everybody except the rulers ends up poor. But if you eliminate the cause of poverty, then you set the people free to produce far more for themselves than the handouts they could get from the State."

"You mean if you replace all existing taxes with collection of site user charges all will be well? Surely it's not as easy as that, Chaka," said Wilson.

"You're absolutely right, Wilson," said Chaka. "For that to work you first need freedom. People must be free."

"That brings us back to square one, Chaka," said Koos. "What is freedom?"

"Simply put, it is being free to pursue your own happiness in any way you like so long as you do not prevent others from doing the same."

"Yes, but as you say, it's not quite as simple as that. So why don't you just tell Koos to read the Freedom Charter?" said Dabulamanzi.

"That's an excellent idea, Dabulamanzi. I think everybody should read it because it is an historic document and makes you think."

"Chaka, do you remember the discussion we had with Petrus a few months ago? I meant to ask you this question then, so I'll ask it now: do you or do you not accept the Charter?" said Dabulamanzi impatiently.

"Well, like all these Bills of Rights it says some good things about civil liberty, but it is too long-winded and ineffective for my liking. And as for economic liberty, I think it sells the people short."

"You must be crazy, Chaka. How could you do any better?"

"The trouble with freedom is that when you define it you limit it. Even if you take all the rights defined in the Charter and all the Bills of Rights in the world put together, they will still not add up to freedom. For freedom is as large as man himself; it is truly a great thing. Now, Koos and Dabulamanzi, tell me, do you not agree that if each man has a right to freedom, all other men have a duty not to take it from him?"

"Of course," they said.

"So if you were to define the duties men owed in respect of their fellows' freedom, they would be free to do everything else?"

"Sounds fine in theory. But wouldn't the list be just as long as the rights?"

"Let's see. For a start, I suppose we all agree that there is a duty on each of us not unlawfully to assault or imprison our fellow men?"

"Sure."

"And likewise not to deprive another of his property or damage it in any way?"

"Yes."

"Nor unlawfully to damage or destroy the good name and reputation of another?"

"Yes."

"And do these duties also apply to the State, which must not only observe them itself but also see that its citizens observe them?"

"Yes, of course."

"And when the State prevents men from living where they choose or performing a trade of their choosing, does it not, in a sense, imprison them?"

"I suppose so."

"So of course all the apartheid restrictions on freedom of movement and speech and assembly must go."

"That's all very well, Chaka," said Sakkie, "But when meetings or the media incite their audiences to violence, that can't be allowed."

"That's quite right, Sakkie," said Chaka, "but can you see that all that would be covered by the three simple duties which we have laid down? So instead of just banning meetings or people or publications, do you agree that the State should have to show in court that otherwise people would probably be deprived of or suffer loss in regard to their liberty or property?"

"That seems fine to me, Chaka," said Dabulamanzi, "although I am sure the legal experts wouldn't like anything so short and simple. But I still don't see why you say the Freedom Charter sells the people short on economic freedom."

"Well, for a start, it insists on a 40-hour working week. So it takes away both my freedom to work a leisurely 20-hour week and eager beaver Wilson's to work his 50-hour week, not to mention some of our taxi-drivers' and builders' 80-hour weeks."

"No, Chaka, you're missing the point. The Charter is trying to protect the people from exploitation. You know the people are so poor and the jobs so few that some of them will work 60 hours a week if they have to, just to get jobs. And even if Anglo American doesn't take advantage of that, there will always be some employers who do."

"So you say that because we are poor we must have our freedom to decide how long we work taken from us? But let us just suppose that men and land were free, apartheid gone, sanctions ended, foreign capital flowing back, the economy booming and jobs plentiful, do you think we would still need that 'protection'? Suppose we had our own jewellers and goldsmiths transforming our diamonds and gold into things of beauty for women the world over. Suppose other industries were processing the other minerals instead of just exporting our ore as if South Africa were one big quarry for the rest of the world. Do you not think our people would be keen to work hard and lift themselves up rather than enjoying this 'protection', however well meant, of the Freedom Charter?"

"Chaka, I find it very hard to believe South Africa could become such a paradise, but even then the people would need this protection for their own good. And as you say, people must spend time with their families enjoying the finer things of life instead of just chasing money."

"Quite so, Dabulamanzi, and you wouldn't catch old Chaka joining in the rat-race. But isn't that what freedom is all about? I mean if people are paying the natural rent — in other words, returning to the community that part of their production which is due to the natural resources of the country — then they would not be interfering with the freedom of others to do the same. So those who were hungry for material goods would own more land and work harder to get there, whereas old Chaka, who likes nothing more than time to talk of these things with young people like you, would own only a small stand on which he could make just enough to keep the hyenas from the door."

"All right, Chaka," said Dabulamanzi, "maybe in this paradise of yours we could have a referendum for the people to decide whether they wanted a 40-hour week or not. But in any case, you are just picking on one little thing in the Freedom Charter. What about nationalising the banks, the mines and the monopolies? What about re-dividing the land amongst those who work it? You are obviously not a capitalist, so surely you must agree these things are good for the people?"

"But that's just the point, Dabulamanzi. By nationalising the monopolies the Freedom Charter is preserving them and denying the people the freedom to compete with them. You see, by collecting the natural rent on land instead of taxing production, you are eliminating the root cause of monopoly. At the same time, as we saw when we spoke of banks, you are encouraging them to return to their true function of providing credit for production, instead of just lending to those who have amassed massive security through non-payment of the natural rent. And again, as we have seen, in order for banks to fulfil this function, the last thing we want is to eliminate competition between them — which is what will happen if we nationalise them.

"And then the mines. Firstly, we must be careful not to destroy a good thing. That's what state intervention did elsewhere — like, for example, in Zambia. When Kaunda nationalised the copper mines they went steadily downhill. Secondly, are you aware that the richer mines already pay up to 80% of profits to the State? In fact, if we look at the levels of tax that more marginal mines have to pay, both in direct taxes and in indirect taxes such as G.S.T., petrol taxes, import duties, and PAYE on employees' earnings, then we will no doubt find that there are many of them which will be forced to close if the gold price drops significantly. In addition, these taxes are preventing many lower-grade deposits from being worked in the first place. Don't forget that collecting the natural rent instead of tax means that, in the case of poorer deposits, the rent in many cases would be nil. So, with no rent or tax to pay, they would be opened, thus creating more jobs and earning valuable foreign exchange. Finally, collection of natural rent on mining land means that there would be no more hoarding of valuable mineral rights. To put it crudely, people sitting on those leases or titles would have to, as they say, do something, or get off the pot! So you see, with collection of rent instead of taxation, you would not need to nationalise the mines, you would not penalise existing mines in any way and, to cap it all, you would encourage many new mines to start. Here again, therefore, collection of rent, instead of state control, points the way to freedom and prosperity."

"Yes, Chaka, but don't tell me you are going to say the same about dividing up the land?"

"If you can show me why not, Dabulamanzi, then I most certainly will not," said Chaka.

"Well, obviously you know the reason, Chaka! The Boers took our land. Then those of our people who were not pushed into the homelands had no choice but to work for the white farmers. How can you justify the present situation where the whites restrict the blacks, who comprise 80% of the population, to 13% of the land?"

"I certainly wouldn't try to justify it, Dabulamanzi, especially since we

72

have agreed that apartheid must go, which means the Group Areas Act must go and blacks can own land anywhere.

"But before we go any further, let us look at what Robert Mugabe did when he came to power in Zimbabwe. Did you know that the 5 000 or 6 000 white-owned farms, which comprised about half the available agricultural land, produced about 80% of the food, while the other half, upon which some 5 000 000 black Zimbabweans lived, produced the rest? Now Mugabe, as we all know, is a socialist, if not a communist. So what did he do? Chase the whites away and give their land to the blacks? Not a bit of it! He encouraged them to stay! Maybe he didn't want the starvation which followed in Angola and Mozambique when the Portuguese left. Likewise in South Africa, the 70 000 white-owned farms produce over 80% of the food while the black homelands and 'independent' states, with a population of some 12 million, produce the rest. And in America only three percent of the workers are on the land, yet they produce enough food for the U.S. and the export market — in fact, they produce too much! So much so that the American Government pays them some $20 billion a year to curb production!"

"No matter what you say about the Freedom Charter, Chaka, the present situation is unjust and the people want action!"

"Yes, Dabulamanzi, but what action? Do you realise that to some extent this Nationalist Government has been doing exactly what the Freedom Charter says?"

"What do you mean, Chaka?" said Dabulamanzi.

"For many years they have been buying white farms and giving them to the homelands. And in many cases it is unfortunately true that those farms which once produced efficiently are now eroded and unproductive."

"Watch out, Chaka! If you're trying to prove whites can farm well and blacks can't? ..."

"Quite the contrary, Dabulamanzi! Even the whites, as shown by the studies of the Free Market Foundation, are beginning to recognise that many black farmers were efficient and worthy competitors of white farmers in the late nineteenth century, especially in the Eastern Cape and Natal. But what it does show, once again, is that misguided efforts by the State to re-distribute land, as well as other wealth, can have exactly the opposite effects to those intended!"

"Very well, Chaka, but no doubt you get the message — action, man! So what exactly would you do about the unjust distribution of land?"

"Hau, my brothers, this is not my day. Now I'm expected to be a farmer as well. Maybe this thing is too difficult to get across!"

"Not at all, Chaka," said Wilson Radebe. "I know exactly what you would say! It's the same story. Everyone can buy land anywhere. All they have to do is pay the natural rent. No doubt with the banks competing fully as you suggest, they would provide credit for some blacks to buy white farms. Maybe some of these Western do-gooders from overseas would like to put their money where their mouths are and put up the funds so I could set up a bank specifically to help black farmers."

"Yes, but before you get carried away Wilson," said Robert Armitage, "remember that most white farmers are relatively efficient and would be able to pay higher rents than the blacks, many of whom would lack the necessary skills and experience to run a farm profitably. Also remember that this 13% black/87% white land ratio ignores the fact that more than half of the 'white' area is non-arable, since much of it is Karoo and semi-desert. Under Chaka's proposals many of these farmers would actually be better off than they are now."

"I know, Robert," said Wilson, "and perhaps I'm better suited to banking in Soweto than in the 'platteland'. But somehow I feel that there would be plenty of cases where black farmers could get going. In fact, it would be a fascinating exercise to see whether, in some areas, black smallholders using co-operative and labour-intensive methods couldn't achieve results on a par with the larger, highly mechanised farms. In any event, I feel that at the end of the day the real farmers amongst both blacks and whites would accept the challenge willingly in the realisation that with equal access to the acquisition of skills, capital and land, the only criteria for success would be ability and energy. No doubt over time there would be a gradual redistribution of land as more blacks bought their own farms. But it would happen through free market forces, not bureaucracy. And it would lead all the time to increasing production, not stagnation. And race would cease to be an issue because every genuine farmer, black or white, would know he had an equal opportunity to get his own 'plaas' in the sun."

"Thank you, Wilson," said Chaka with a sigh of relief. "It remains only to point out that for this system to work, all these farmers would have to have confidence in the fairness of the system on which the determination of rentals was based. It would have to be open, public, related to objective market forces, subject to appeal and administered without fear or favour by honest men."

"Yes, Chaka," said Robert Armitage, "and that brings us to an aspect of freedom to which you referred rather disparagingly — I mean the Bill of Rights to protect the individual in the Constitution."

"Yes, Robert," said Chaka. "Whether you had an elaborate Bill of Rights in your constitution or relied on the enforcement of the simple duties I mentioned, you would still have to have judges who were above politics and dedicated only to the upholding of justice."

"That's where we differ, Robert," said Sakkie. "You people in the Democratic Party think that's enough. We say, yes, an independent judiciary and protection of the individual from discrimination are good and necessary. But to ensure that the minority groups are truly free they must have an effective share in the government of the country. That's why we insist on power-sharing. Now what do you say to that, Chaka?"

"Sakkie, the trouble with power-sharing is that the people think, as Dabulamanzi said, that it's just another device to preserve white privilege. Also, some Ministers talk of 'sharing power without losing control', which of course destroys its credibility in the eyes of the people."

"I should think so!" said Dabulamanzi approvingly — for a change.

"Yes, but I'm talking about the genuine article, Chaka — not about tricks," said Sakkie. "Let us say, for example, that we were all to agree on these principles which you say would unleash economic progress and opportunity for all, and that we were all competing on a level economic playground. By your own admission this would sweep away the root causes of discrimination and injustice against the people. Would you still say then that power-sharing would not work?"

"Well," answered Chaka, "strictly speaking power-sharing would not be necessary because these very principles would not only remove the barriers to black advancement, they would also preserve for whites the opportunity to be full and free players in the game — on level terms. However, if whites were prepared to go along with these ideas, then it follows that blacks might accept a form of genuine power-sharing in return. Even Dabulamanzi here would no doubt recognise that 'in the real world' you don't get something for nothing. That means that the whites are unlikely to surrender their privileges and power, ill-gotten though they may be, without getting something in return. So yes, I suppose you have a point. That could be the basis of a deal."

"Chaka, before you presume on my willingness to do deals with the apartheid-merchants, would you mind just kindly telling me whether power-sharing has ever worked in history and, if so, what form it took?" said Dabulamanzi with more than a tinge of sarcasm in his voice.

"Aikona, Dabulamanzi! Listen my brother, one minute you expect me to be a farmer, the next an expert in the history of constitutional law! Give me a break!"

"Yes of course, Chaka," said Dabulamanzi sweetly, "provided you admit you've been talking nonsense all the time."

"You can be the judge of that, Dabulamanzi," said Chaka. "But tell me first, have you heard of Magna Carta?"

"Of course — but that was just an agreement between an English king and his land barons that he would not push them around whenever he felt like it."

"And the Great Reform Act of 1832?"

"That was just the co-opting by the English aristocracy of the capitalists and bourgeoisie into the system."

"And the Reform Acts of 1876 and 1884?"

"They just co-opted the petty bourgeoisie and finally the workers."

"Wouldn't you say, then, that the British Constitution was one long series of power-sharing deals between Crown, landowners, industrialists and workers?"

"That's one way of looking at it, I suppose."

"Now, Dabulamanzi, what about the United States, Canada and Switzerland? Aren't all these power-sharing deals between large states and small ones, French and English, and French, German and Italian?"

"Sure, but what's that got to do with us?"

"I'm coming to that. But first tell me now — don't you think that Lebanon was a far happier place before the Jordanians chased the P.L.O. out of Jordan and, in effect, into Lebanon? Do you remember that then Lebanon had a power-sharing arrangement between the various religious and cultural groups such as Christians, Druse and Muslims? And that, whatever its imperfections, Lebanon was relatively peaceful and far more prosperous than now?"

"Yes, but it favoured the dominant Christian minority."

"Quite so. But before it had a chance to adapt to the growing awareness and power of the Muslim communities the P.L.O. burst onto the scene and chaos ensued. Now, let us look at power-sharing the other way round. Dabulamanzi, I'm sure you have noticed how much strife there is in those countries where ethnic, cultural or religious minorities have *not* been given an effective share in government. This applies in more than twenty countries all over the world — for example, Sri Lanka; Fiji; Turkey; Iraq; Iran with the Kurds; Spain, with its Basques; Ulster, with the Catholics; Chad and Sudan, with Muslim vs Christian; and so on. Does this not at least suggest that winner-take-all democracy needs some modification in these situations?"

"Yes, but I still think you haven't given us a close enough example of power-sharing for it to make sense to us here in South Africa."

"That may be so, but remember, all I was trying to show was that those countries which have worked out some kind of power-sharing arrangement via peaceful negotiation have been far more successful than those where the minority groups have been ignored. And although I can't give you any examples close to us in time, there is one which, although it occurred thousands of years ago, may be more relevant than we think."

"What's that, Chaka?" asked Alfred Nkosi.

"I'm thinking of the early Roman patricians who founded the city and established its dominance over the surrounding tribes of Latium. As a result of their success, members of the other tribes came to live nearby, but outside the walls of the city. In time they came to serve in the Roman legions and contributed to the greatness of Rome in much the same way that we blacks have flocked to the 'white' cities of South Africa and helped build up the most prosperous economy in Africa. In due course these Latin tribesmen or plebeians began to demand full equality as citizens of Rome. Needless to say, the patricians were loath to let them in because they were outnumbered and would have been swamped. They saw themselves as the custodians and founders of the virtues which had made Rome great and, of course, they didn't want to become underlings. But the plebeians were insistent.

"So the Romans, patrician and plebeian alike, had to make a choice: either they fought each other, in which case Rome would be destroyed and we would probably never even have heard of it, or they could work out a compromise and prosper. Which in fact is what they did. By a long series of changes to their constitution, they evolved a system whereby the plebeian legislature had power to pass certain laws which previously only the patrician Senate of Rome could do. More importantly, however, the executive power was shared between the two groups. Thus the great magistracies of Rome — the consuls, praetors, quaestors, aediles and so on — often comprised equal numbers of patricians and plebeians. In some cases special magistrates, such as the tribunes, were appointed with powers of veto to protect the plebeians' interests.

"Over the years the distinction between patrician and plebeian gradually lost its importance as the plebeians became fully integrated into the fabric of Rome."

"Chaka, you're not seriously suggesting we model the future South Africa on the Roman Republic?" said Dabulamanzi.

"Not at all, Dabulamanzi. You see, one thing is certain. If black and white ever seriously negotiate a new dispensation in South Africa, it will be different from anything that has ever happened elsewhere. The reason for that is simple. Power-sharing can take many different forms. It might take the form of cantons as proposed by Frances Kendall and Leon Louw in *The Solution*, or the geographical federation proposed by the old PFP, or the federal-confederal constitution first proposed by the now-defunct New Republic Party, or a mixture of all three — or something entirely different. The mechanisms of power-sharing will be subject to one thing only, and that is the desire of all South Africans to hammer out a peaceful framework which takes into account both their fears and their aspirations. Given that desire and the realisation of the enormous potential that exists here, I am sure that South Africans, working together instead of fighting each other, can go on to create a powerhouse of prosperity and freedom that will be an inspiration for the rest of Africa if not the whole world."

"It may do, Chaka," said Dabulamanzi, "but a moment ago you said that strictly speaking power-sharing wouldn't be necessary once members of all groups were assured of equal opportunity. So perhaps you had better leave off trying to justify power-sharing by reference to hard cases elsewhere in the world and get back to principle. Strictly speaking then, what is the justification for power-sharing?"

"Dabulamanzi, you always go for my weak points. But fortunately, you will remember, it's not my idea." Then, turning to Sakkie, Chaka said, "Over to you."

"Sure," said Sakkie confidently. "Let's get back to our ideal of freedom which you described so neatly. So far we've glossed over the fact that it appears to conflict with the need for government. Don't forget, my people were trekking away from the government of the Dutch East India Company long before they went on the Great Trek away from the British Government of the Cape Colony. We just assumed that democracy was the same as freedom. It's not. It's a form of government. The reason people have come to equate it with freedom is that it is supposed to be government by consent. In other words, if the people agree to what that government decides it does not take away from their freedom because they have agreed to it of their own free will. Incidentally, let us not forget that democracy means rule by the people. That means the entire 'people' coming together to take decisions. In some of the old Greek city states, early American colonies, and small Swiss cantons this actually happened; in fact, in some cantons, it still does happen. What we mean by democracy nowadays is in fact representative democracy. The people choose their representatives and it is assumed that the people thereby give their consent to what their representatives decide. Needless to say, this is not always so in practice!

"Then there is another question. If 51% of 'the people' — and it can be considerably less than 51% if only a small proportion of voters bother to go to the polls — or their representatives want one thing and the other 49% are opposed, why on earth do we proceed with the make-believe that 'the people' are being governed by their consent if nearly half of them don't want it? This in fact is the 'tyranny of the majority'. Well, the constitutional theorists have a partial answer to that. They say that you can assume that a government comprising only 51% of the representatives of the people will act in the interests of the people as a whole because of the 'sanction of alternative government'. In other words, they will be thrown out at the next election if they go against the wishes of the people as a whole.

"Now, this works in homogeneous communities like, say, England or Holland. But when you have relatively deep and permanent divisions in your electorates, the tyranny of the majority becomes just that. This means that an ethnic, cultural or religious minority no longer enjoys the benefits of democracy. It becomes politically emasculated or, if you like, enslaved. Its members are governed without consent and are therefore no longer free. The majority can, and does, ride roughshod time and again over the wishes and interests of the minority. And it can do this without transgressing any of the barriers against discrimination which may be included in the constitution.

"To some extent, therefore, I take Robert's point. The Nationalist Party appealed exclusively to Afrikaners, and once it got the bulk of them into its fold, the English, let alone the blacks, were, for decades after 1948, governed without consent. Chaka mentioned a moment ago other minorities tyrannised under winner-take-all forms of democracy. Now, it's all very well to say people shouldn't vote or form parties along these lines, but the fact is, they do, all over the world. It is even more futile to argue that, were it not for apartheid, they would not have done so in South Africa. The fact is, they would probably do so now and, more to the point, the majority of whites are convinced they will. This is why they do not wish, as they see it, to surrender their freedom to 'the tyranny of the majority'. And if the rest of the world persists in pushing them into it, then I'm afraid the strife that will ensue here will make the bloodshed that has occurred in Ulster and Sri Lanka and elsewhere look like a tea party."

Sakkie continued: "Evidence that politicians in winner-take-all systems will exploit and exacerbate anti-minority feelings was discussed by *The Economist* in this article dealing with Sikh-Hindu violence. I brought this along with me, because I thought something on these lines might crop up in our discussion.

"Unscrupulous politicians have discovered that it is easy to provoke a riot amid so much bad temper. First you take advantage of (and sometimes even arrange) an 'incident': someone in your community gets murdered, a shrine is defiled, a woman is raped. Then you send a small group of people, probably the thugs you keep on retainer for your protection racket, to stir up the poor and the angry in your community over the insult they have suffered. If it is a serious affair, people may be bused in from other parts of town or from the countryside. The gang may also get some weapons together – sticks, knives, kerosene. Having picked out some shops and houses belonging to the other side, the gang attacks. The other side fights back and your riot goes ahead as planned. If you are a member of the ruling party in your state or town, you may be able to arrange in advance for the police not to intervene. The riots in Delhi after Indira Gandhi's murder undoubtedly included some politically backed violence. All the investigations by Indian civil rights groups concluded that local and national Congress party leaders helped to organise some of the killing. Men on scooters identified Sikh shops and houses, in some areas marking them with chalk. Truckloads of young men were brought in from neighbouring parts of Haryana state. All over town, mobs attacked in the same way, with the same weapons (first iron bars, then kerosene), which suggests planning. Eye-witness statements accused local Congress party officials of leading mobs. The police kept out, and the army was called in only after two days. The Congress party is not the only one whose members do this sort of thing. Riots in Hyderabad have been stirred up by both fundamentalist Muslim and right-wing Hindu parties, and in Bombay by the Hindu Shiv Sena (Army of Shiva). Why do the politicians do it? Religious or caste-based parties benefit from riots, particularly when their supporters have begun deserting to broader-based parties. The Shiv Sena, which in the early 1980's looked like a spent force, returned to prominence after the Bombay riots in 1984, and now runs the city. A majority party which takes a strong anti-minority line will often be strengthened by riots, which vividly remind the majority how much they dislike the minority."

79

Putting the paper down, Sakkie said, "The alternative is to take account of the reasonable fears of the minority groups by adapting the democratic form of government so as to ensure that the minorities have an effective share of government at the executive as well as legislative levels. This is what power-sharing is all about. And it will be necessary to continue with it until the minorities see that their fears are groundless."

Sakkie paused at last, whereupon Robert Armitage spoke up. "I find it interesting to hear a Nat justifying power-sharing after all the years in which they enjoyed a winner-take-all situation in the white electorate, and although I agree with a lot of what you say, there are two pre-conditions for power-sharing which are sadly lacking. Firstly, the major groups and parties must recognise that they have no hope of gaining or maintaining dominance. Secondly, we need a climate of reconciliation right from grass-roots up to the top before such a thing can work."

"Well, you all know I am a radical," said Dabulamanzi. "But whereas in the unrest a few years ago we all thought the People's Government was a few weeks away, it soon became clear that the white regime could hang in for years, or even decades if it wanted to. That is one of the reasons why, now that F.W. de Klerk has opened the way to peaceful negotiations, most of us are prepared to give them a chance. The problem seems to be with the whites who are now giving their support to the CP and the AWB."

"I'm not so sure about that, Dabulamanzi," said Koos. "I think a lot of whites are only registering protest votes against the poor state of the economy and F.W. de Klerk's failure to tell us where he is taking us with his power-sharing and what the advantages of it would be. At the moment people see only the dangers. If he were to do that, and the black leaders really do negotiate, I am sure the majority of whites would support him right up to the hilt."

"Well, let's hope he does that soon," said Chaka. "Because two things are certain. If whites and blacks go on fighting for domination instead of co-operating, this country will destroy itself. But if they work together, whites and blacks can make this one of the fastest-growing and most prosperous countries in the world."

10 WHO OWNS THE LAND AND HOW

Georgii Quinti Anno Sexto, I, who won the River field,
Am fortified with title-deeds, attested, signed and sealed,
Guaranteeing me, my assigns, my executors and heirs,
All sorts of powers and profits which – are neither mine nor theirs!

Rudyard Kipling

The earth is the Lord's and the fullness thereof.

Psalm 24

Talk about freedom ended when Alfred's wife and daughters served food. Instead they spoke of sport and argued about how many gold medals South Africa would have won had she been allowed to compete in the '88 Olympic Games. Koos and Sakkie also said that while South Africa's old rugby chief 'Doc' Craven may not have done the right thing in talking to the A.N.C., it was high time South Africa re-entered the rugby world. Afrikaners playing rugby in other African countries and overseas would be a major factor in softening racist attitudes of right-wing whites, they said. Dabulamanzi was for continued isolation until 'liberation', but agreed with the others that after liberation, sport could be a major force for unity in this games-mad country.

When Robert asked Alfred whether he had taken advantage of reform to buy his house, the talk turned to land tenure. Koos asked Dabulamanzi how land could be 're-divided amongst those who work it' as proposed by the Freedom Charter.

"By taking from those who have too much and giving to those who have none, of course!" said Dabulamanzi.

"And will they hold the land just like the Whites do now?" asked Wilson Radebe.

"Of course!" said Dabulamanzi. "There will be no discrimination against the people after liberation!"

"Do you realise, then, that you will just be creating another class of land-owning capitalists who cheat the people?" asked Wilson.

For a moment Dabulamanzi glared at Wilson in speechless anger. How could this upstart banker say the Freedom Charter would make the same mistakes as capitalism? he thought.

Quickly taking advantage of Dabulamanzi's silence, Wilson explained that, if this new class of landowners did not have to pay a site user charge, they too could be a drag on everybody else. They could either lease their land to tenants and live off the rent, or they could be idle and not use it fully or at all while waiting to sell it at a profit later. On the other hand, if everybody was free to buy where they wanted — if, in other words, the Group Areas Act had gone completely — the collection of the natural rent would soon lead to a plentiful supply of land so that all those who could put land to good use could get some. He also showed how this would avoid the economic collapse which would be caused by the expense and disruption, not to mention violence, of a wholesale 'people's redistribution'. It would happen naturally over time, aided by the 'invisible hand' of a free market in land.

At this point Robert Armitage said, "You know, what interests me in all this talk about land is not that blacks want the same rights to land as whites. I'm sure I also would if I were in your shoes, even though the traditional African land system is based on communal tenure. But people seem to think that the so-called right of absolute private ownership, or freehold, which the whites have now, is both the only system worth having and the only system that has ever existed in this country."

"Go on, Robert, tell me when was it ever any different," said Wilson. "I thought all the whites did was push us aside and then start buying and selling it amongst themselves."

Robert, who as well as being a dry accountant had made a study of the history of the early Dutch, British and Trekker systems of land tenure, said, "Although Van Riebeeck soon recognised the need for individual land ownership if the Cape was to produce enough food for the Dutch fleets, the Dutch freehold, unlike the British, was usually saddled with conditions. So when the first whites got their land in 1657 they were, after three years, to pay 'such reasonable taxes' as the Dutch East India Company saw fit to place on their land. They also had to sell all their produce to the Company at its prices and do guard duty at the Company's defences.

"Later on the Company discovered that farmers were grazing their cattle inland, so in 1714 it made them pay 12 riksdollars a year in recognition of the loan of these lands to them, or one-tenth of the harvest if they grew crops. Yet the free burghers still used vacant Company land. So in 1732, a fifteen-year leasehold, called quitrent, for 24 riksdollars a year was brought in. Under this system the farmers were afraid to improve their farms as they did not know if their leases would be renewed after 15 years. In 1743, therefore, the Company provided that these farms could be converted into freehold at rentals which could be higher or lower than 24 riksdollars according to whether they were 'more valuable' or whether it was a hardship when the rent was increased from 12 to 24 riksdollars."

"It seems as if they had something very much like what we've been talking about, Robert," said Wilson. "There was no withholding of land from use so as to sell later at a profit — and the Company collected a site-value-based rent."

"In theory, yes, Wilson, but in practice not," said Robert. "The younger sons of the trekboer families went off into the dry interior and got themselves new farms without too much difficulty. The Company was slow to catch up with them and many of them did not bother to pay the rent. So much so that when the British thought they were doing the farmers a favour in 1813 by allowing them to change their loan farms to perpetual quitrent, the trekboers were not interested. This was no doubt partly because, although this new way of holding land meant it could no longer be taken away from them by the Government, they had to pay an increased yearly rent of up to 250 riksdollars. But the real reason was that the loan farms were in fact being bought and sold and even subdivided without the Company or Government keeping track of it.

"Later on, because of the long delays in granting land under this system, the local landdrosts, or magistrates, started granting land unlawfully on a request basis with the annual quitrent being fixed at between 30 and 50 riksdollars, or about 1% of the estimated value."

"And what happened when the British Settlers landed in the Eastern Cape in 1820? Were they given land on freehold?" asked Chaka.

"No, they were given land on perpetual quitrent," said Robert. "Freehold sales began in 1843, but in 1856 the Cape Parliament restored the quitrent system. They later sold land on quitrent by public auction. This meant that the Government collected revenue both on sale of the land and by way of annual rent."

"Meanwhile, the Boers didn't like the British attempts to tighten up the system of land tenure and collect rental from them, so they left the Colony on the Great Trek," said Sakkie.

"Yes, that was one of the reasons the Voortrekkers left but, interestingly enough, although the first republican government in Natal gave their burghers land on freehold, they still had to pay a yearly rent of 12 riksdollars on farms of 1 000 morgen (2 100 acres) or more 'for the protection they received in regard to their lands'.

"In the Transvaal and Orange Free State the same principles applied. All citizens could claim a farm of 3 000 morgen and early trekkers could even claim two farms. As regards rent, however, it was only in 1876 that the Free State got around to imposing a land tax of two shillings per 220 acres. The constitution of the South African Republic in the Transvaal allowed the Government to levy a tax of between six and 40 riksdollars on all farms 'for the protection of such property.' The rent was payable only after the farm was officially inspected to fix the exact boundaries after final title was given. In the meantime the farmers held their land on the basis of a description of the farm which they lodged at the landdrost's office. The landdrost gave the farmer an extract, or Uittreksel, of this record. In some of the outlying districts the government was slow to finish the inspections, so that for years land was held, or bought and sold, on the basis of these Uittreksels. In the meantime the farmers paid no rent and sometimes delayed the inspections so as to continue avoiding rent."

"This is all very interesting," said Alfred, "but why is there no trace of these land rentals today, and why are you telling us all this? It could hardly seem less relevant to today."

"On the contrary, Alfred," said Robert. "It is very important to crack on the head this idea that land ownership without any obligation to one's fellow man is deeply embedded in the tradition of South Africa. What I said shows that for the first two hundred years and more of White settlement there was widespread recognition by the colonial and republican governments that land ownership carried with it the obligation to pay some kind of rental to the community. That, plus the Black African tradition of communal tenure, means that all South Africans who know their own history will be much more ready to agree that land ownership by individuals naturally carries with it certain basic duties.

"But as regards your first question, Alfred, I suppose the answer is that the discovery of gold and diamonds in the second half of the nineteenth century opened up much easier sources of revenue for all the governments in the region. It was easier for President Kruger to tax the unpopular Uitlander gold mines than to chase his Boer farmers for land rent. After the Boer War South Africa came quickly into line with British and American practice where land rent was ignored.

"But before that, the failure of the governments to collect meaningful land rents led to widespread speculation. One British official complained that the speculators followed on the heels of advancing British armies like plagues of grasshoppers. Another complained that Natal, with a population of a third-rate English town, suffered a land shortage in the midst of 12 million acres.

"The historian De Kiewiet tells how, as early as 1851, when the Colony of Natal was less than ten years old, there was very little Crown land at a convenient distance from Durban. When the Government tried in 1857 to encourage immigrants by paying their fares, only 300 arrived and of the 1,36 million acres they were given, most ended up in the hands of speculators.

"In the Republic the practice of giving 6 000-acre farms to every man meant that by the time the British first annexed the Transvaal in 1877, there was no longer a farm for every man and his sons. Even in the early years of the

Trek there were blocks of privately owned land of 200 000 to 300 000 acres. In 1854 there was an almost unbroken line of 200 farms from Winburg to Harrismith held by absentee owners."

Now Dabulamanzi, who had been listening intently, spoke up. "That's quite right, Robert, I've also read De Kiewiet. But do you know what the most important thing is that he said about our land?"

"I don't know, Dabulamanzi, but I was just going to say that he made the point that the careless way in which the Cape and Natal colonies allowed such vast areas of land to fall into the hands of speculators and absentee landowners meant that the stream of settlers from Britain, who had no money to pay the speculators, passed South Africa by and went to Australia and North America instead, where they were able to build their future on land made freely available by the authorities there. He says those countries benefited from wave after wave of hungry hard-working immigrants who challenged the habits of the earlier settlers with their energy, new ideas and new methods. Had they come to South Africa things would have been very different."

"Trust you to emphasise that!" laughed Dabulamanzi. "No, I weep no tears for the failure of whites to settle properly the land they grabbed from us. What De Kiewiet also pointed out was that the lands which the whites claimed were empty, had only been vacated temporarily by their inhabitants who were hiding from the Zulu and Matabele impis.

"As soon as the Boers broke the power of the Zulus and Matabele, the other tribes came out of hiding, only to find that farms had been established over their kraals. So they became squatters and were allowed to stay only because they paid rent to the white landowners or worked for them."

'Yes, I've heard these arguments before, Dabulamanzi," said Sakkie. "No doubt the historians are going to have a field day arguing over what to tell our children in years to come. But I don't know what good quarrelling about the past is going to do. The question is, where do we go from here? Is there a way we can solve the land problem peacefully, or must our people start fighting all over again?"

"Maybe, Sakkie," said Dabulamanzi, "but first I want to put right some of the ideas whites seem to have about traditional African land tenure. Robert, for example, spoke of communal tenure. Well, we're fed up with government officials and academics blaming 'communal tenure' for the poor state of agriculture in the so-called black homelands. What they conveniently forget, as has been shown in a book published recently by one of our graduate researchers at Wits, Essy Letsoalo, is that the failings of 'communal tenure' are due to the complete distortion of our traditional system by the whites who took away the real power of our chiefs and instead made them puppets of apartheid. For instance, she shows that under our system, when a family had been allocated land by the chief it could not be taken away. In other words, we had all the security of tenure we needed to look after our land properly and improve it.

"She also shows how title to land was related to use of the land and to membership of the tribe. Only when a family decided to sever ties with the tribe did the land cease to belong to the family. Furthermore, the system was flexible and showed every sign of changing with the times. One example of this was the speed with which blacks responded to market opportunities created by the discovery of gold and diamonds. In several areas black farmers even out-produced and out-performed whites.

"Moreover," continued Dabulamanzi, turning to Robert, "you may be interested to hear that she goes on to say that tribal tenure was not really communal. She says it's closer to the old English system of common lands."

"That's absolutely fascinating, Dabulamanzi," said Robert, excited for once. "I had no idea that was so. But this raises a most interesting question: given the flexibility which you say African tribal tenure once had, would it have remained in harmony with nature or would it have repeated 'the tragedy of the commons'?"

"How do you mean?"

"Well, at the time of the Agricultural and Industrial Revolutions, England had reached the point where new discoveries meant the old methods used by farmers under the commons system had to make way for modern ways of producing more with less labour. In time, work opportunities for those not needed on the land arose in the new mines and factories. All of this was quite natural. It also meant that the productivity of both farming and urban land rose in leaps and bounds, giving rise to what we have called natural rent. What was quite wrong was that instead of capturing this for the benefit of all via some kind of user charge on the value of the land, the English government allowed those who owned the land to benefit from these developments for no equivalent input, and the yeomen and proud peasants of England became poor and landless. Shakespeare alludes to this in *Richard III* when the dying John of Gaunt chides the king: 'Landlord of England art thou, not king'. And that was well before the major land enclosures took place."

"You raise a good question, Robert, because the natural development of tribal tenure was cut short before it had to deal with the question of rent. Because land was abundant, the idea that some members of the tribe could benefit from much more productive land never really arose. The only 'rent' the people paid was to members of the tribe, although I suppose you could say that membership carried certain duties such as military service to help defend the tribal lands. But had commercial and industrial development taken place, the chiefs would still have retained the function of allocating land for these purposes as well. It is not too far-fetched to think that the tribal elders would soon have seen the need for some kind of payment to the tribe for the use of those lands that were obviously much more productive than others. One justification for saying

86

this is that title to land was granted only if the land was to be used. Another justification is the natural harmony of the tribal structure which made divorce, illegitimacy and poverty almost unheard of. It is hard to think that this structure would have allowed some members to acquire great wealth by dispossessing others of their tribal birthright."

"We'll never know, of course," chipped in Robert, "but one could also argue that the tribal chiefs would have acted exactly like the old feudal lords and grabbed all the land for themselves as soon as they could see the wealth being generated by new farming methods, industry and commerce. The only thing that can stop this greed is a true knowledge of the harmony of the economic organism. But maybe the tribal chiefs and elders had this knowledge, in which case your description of how the system would have operated may well be correct."

"Okay," came in Sakkie, trying to get the conversation back to present-day realities, "but how do we solve the land problem peacefully, or must we fight all over again?"

"Well," replied Dabulamanzi, "obviously we have to do away with all restrictions preventing blacks from buying land in their own country. Then, I suppose, we have to admit that since not all can own the same quality land, this user charge thing of Chaka's is probably the ideal 'equaliser'. I mean, if it worked properly it would achieve equal access to land inasmuch as those on inferior land would not be at a disadvantage, because those with better land would be paying the market rate to the community for that advantage."

"That's right, Dabulamanzi," said Chaka. "What you and Robert have said is very interesting, and if we listen to you both carefully we can avoid the mistakes both our peoples made in the past."

"How's that, old man?" asked Dabulamanzi.

"Well, it seems our African system of land tenure was strong in that it emphasised use of land and did not allow a man to exclude others from land just because he was the 'owner' even if he did not use it. The white system, as it developed in practice, gave landowners the security of tenure they needed to improve their land but not the incentive. In fact, by taxing them if they worked the land, and by not collecting the rent, it encouraged them to do nothing and just hold it for speculation."

"Yes, Chaka," said Alfred. "But what if the government had developed the idea of land rents we were talking about earlier?"

"Well, I suppose the farmers would only have taken land they could use properly. And when you don't take more of something than you need, the other man gets a chance. In South Africa, this 'other man' could have been either the European immigrant who had to go elsewhere, or one of our own people, who could have stayed on his land instead of being pushed aside by whites. The 'land-hunger' of the whites in the nineteenth century was made much worse because of speculation, which resulted from the failure of the colonial and republican governments to collect the rents. So, if they had collected proper rents via user charges or in some other way, South Africa would have had a lot more white immigrants and a lot less conflict over land between the tribes and the white settlers."

"Yes, but where does all this get us, Chaka?" asked Dabulamanzi.

"Do you agree that we have found both the strengths and the weaknesses in the early land tenure systems of black and white in South Africa?"

"Yes, of course."

"So that if we leave the weak and take the strong from both and put them together, we will have something that is both strong and new and yet still rooted in our own history?"

"How so?"

"Well if we take our traditional African emphasis on use without speculation, and the white idea of security of tenure via formalised title registered in a deeds office, won't that be better?"

"Yes, but not good enough!" said Dabulamanzi.

"Quite so," said Chaka, "and what would be missing?"

"Well, you would have to take the old idea of quitrents and land dues, but instead of the half-baked, half-hearted way in which the old colonial and trekker governments applied them you would have to do it properly," said Dabulamanzi.

"Exactly, Dabulamanzi," said Chaka. "So we would have a strong, clear and fair system which was both new as well as rooted in, and drawn from, the history of our own people here in South Africa."

"I suppose so," said Dabulamanzi.

"Do you see now why we don't have to slavishly follow foreign ideas of capitalism or socialism but merely look at our own history to revolutionise our system of land tenure?"

"Yes."

"And would this not at the same time sweep away the errors of the past without bloodshed and lay the foundation for a free, fair and dynamic future?"

"I suppose so, Chaka, but it sounds too good to be true," said Dabulamanzi.

"Well, if that's the only problem, Dabulamanzi, then that's good news," said Wilson, "because here we have discovered something that is radical enough for you, and fair enough for me. At the same time, at last, we will have something in South Africa that we have found for ourselves, for our own future, from our own past."

Dabulamanzi nodded briefly and bade farewell, followed at last by the others who gave Chaka a lift home at the same time. Alfred stood outside a moment wondering how the 'trial' was going, for he knew Dabulamanzi would give a full report to Petrus and Vusi and the other young radicals and that these ideas were being keenly debated in the township.

11 WHY "TURBULENT" TUTU?

The land shall not be sold forever: for the land is mine; for ye are strangers and sojourners with me.
And in all the land of your possession ye shall grant a redemption for the land.

Leviticus 25: 23-24

The next morning Alfred went to see Chaka at his house. "I have been talking to the priest who was with Wilson Radebe when you spoke on banking."

"Oh! you mean Kazamulu," said Chaka. "He didn't say very much."

"That's probably because he has to talk so much in his job as it is. Also, perhaps, because he is a little unusual in that he is neither the hyperactive politically outspoken type of priest like his Archbishop Desmond Tutu, nor the church-mouse type. In any case, when he heard you would be at home this morning, he said he'd like to see you again."

Sure enough, Kazamulu arrived a minute later saying, "I was interested in the things you talked about, and have discussed them at length with Wilson. I know you say you are not interested in politics; neither am I as such. But many of my brothers in the Church are worried when the people say we are collaborators because we are not active enough in the struggle. Now, I have no problem with my brothers when they speak out against the obvious injustices of apartheid, which I do myself. However, I worry when they go further and propound political solutions or actions which would lead to violence. Our Archbishop, Desmond Tutu, says many things which are popular with our people but which infuriate whites. But even he has admitted he knows nothing about economics. In fact, he has asked for help from businessmen in addressing the problem of poverty. So this has led me to think again and again about what Jesus meant when he said: 'Render unto Caesar that which is Caesar's and unto God that which is God's'."

"Yes, and what came to mind when you did that, Kazamulu?" asked

Chaka.

"Well, I think in the first place Jesus was telling his disciples not to worry about material matters like money and taxes, or about political power, all of which are pretty paltry things compared with the real riches with which he has endowed Mankind. But in another sense his words raise in my mind the question 'What is Caesar's?'. Now, what you seem to be saying is that, insofar as the natural working of the economy is concerned, the natural rent of land is what people should be rendering to Caesar, not taxes. Is this right?"

"Yes, but you put it better than I could, Kazamulu," said Chaka.

"Does this mean, then, that we in the Church should be studying economics in order to point people in the right direction? If so, we shall have precious little time left over for our real task of tending His flock."

"Quite so, Kazamulu. Like you, I have no problem with the Church speaking out against injustice and violence. What's more, if the Church succeeds in its real task, which is spiritual upliftment, its criticisms should be enough to spur men to seek real justice. But, again like you, I think that when the Church goes one step further and propounds solutions, it is falling into the typical error made by Western critics of capitalism."

"Which is?"

"It is to assume that because 'capitalism' seems always to include poverty along with progress, that which is thought to be the only alternative, namely socialism or communism, must be better. But this is typical of the polarised type of thinking of this day and age.

"For instance, if Islam is good, then all other religions are bad, or if the arms race is wrong, then disarmament must be good, or if the previous distinctions between men and women in society were unjust, then all distinctions must be removed, and so on."

"And I suppose you would add to that, if white rule is wrong, black rule must be right," said Alfred.

"Yes, that's the sort of thing I'm talking about. But the list is endless. We could go on all night," said Chaka.

"So you don't go along with the social gospel or Liberation Theology?" asked Kazamulu.

"Not at all. As I said before, the Church is right to stand up against injustice. And it is true to say that when it doesn't, as has happened from time to time all over the world, it becomes part and parcel of an unjust establishment. Now, although the political and economic pronouncements of churchmen here and elsewhere have sometimes been debatable, the Church should always be taken seriously when it points to basic wrongs in society. For example, the Bishops said before the last British election that Mrs Thatcher had not addressed the fundamental problem of poverty in Britain, and the Catholic Bishops in the U.S. said much the same thing when Reagan stood for his second term of office. Well, they were right, because in neither country has poverty been approached properly. And this is the sort of thing which thinking people in those countries, including politicians, economists and businessmen, should take seriously."

"Hang on a minute, Chaka!" said Alfred. "With due respect to my friend Kazamulu here, why do we have to treat their opinions on these matters so seriously? Haven't we agreed that they do not necessarily know any more about politics or economics than the rest of us?"

"Yes, but first of all, Alfred, please remember we are not talking about their political ideas but about fundamental injustice. In the second place, as I explained to the people at Soweto Suzy's the other day, the Church, in the natural order of things, acts at the level of government. We called this the fourth level in the hierarchy of mankind, with the first three levels making up the economic organism. So if those who lead the Church are men of integrity and true devotion, then they are right to point out basic wrongs, and when they do so, they speak with proper authority at the level of government. That is why when the spiritual leaders of government in this broad sense speak like this, the temporal leaders in government, and all the rest of us, ought to listen."

"Yes, I suppose so," said Alfred.

"Perhaps," said Kazamulu, "we should be thankful that despite attempts at manipulation from all sides, the churches in this country are still a force for peaceful, rather than violent, change. To their ranks we can now probably add the Dutch Reformed Church, which has at last rejected apartheid and asked for forgiveness for condoning it in the past. No wonder that the ultra right-wingers are trying to set up their own apartheid Churches."

"Yes, so the turbulent relationship between P.W. Botha in his Tuynhuis and our Archbishop in his Cathedral a few metres away was very much what one would have expected at that stage of affairs," said Alfred.

"That's right. But if F.W. takes the bull by the horns and gets our people to the conference table, I am sure that my Archbishop would no longer be a thorn in his flesh. On the contrary, I think De Klerk would soon see our Cathedral, standing as it does a stone's throw away from Parliament, symbolising the proper place of the Church as a bulwark against violence and injustice in the State. No longer would he have the remotest excuse for hinting that the Church has betrayed reform. Far from it. We would be his most powerful ally against those who might continue to promote or condone violence."

"And if Tutu, to cap it all, calls off the boycott brigade, then indeed 'the wolf also shall dwell with the lamb'," said Chaka.

"In the meantime, Chaka, do you think churchmen like Archbishop Tutu are right to be so outspoken?" asked Alfred.

"Yes, except that it would help if they understood that the cause of poverty lies deeper than apartheid. For example, it would be much better if they called for collection of natural rent instead of boycotts and disinvestment. We have shown that if you don't collect rent you will have poverty. As Henry George said in his book *Progress and Poverty*, 'you may have progress, especially if you do not otherwise interfere with the workings of the free market. But with it, if you do not collect rent, you will always have poverty.' That is why, even in boom times, the prosperous West cannot get rid of poverty. Like Brer Rabbit's Tarbaby, it just sticks to the system."

"Yes, but what did George mean when he said, '...otherwise interfere with the free market', Chaka?"

"Well, Kazamulu, you know, those who argue that the Government must leave almost everything to the free market forget about a free market in the most important thing of all!"

"Surely you don't mean land, Chaka?"

"Yes, why not?"

"Well, Chaka, people buy and sell land freely now — apart from the Group Areas Act, that is."

"But Kazamulu, suppose St Mary's Cathedral is expropriated for a new fire station and Archbishop Tutu wants to use the compensation to buy land for another cathedral in the centre of Johannesburg. Let us say that his agent quietly manages to buy the one-acre city block that he needs — all except for one little piece of ground, 500 m^2 or one-eighth of an acre. Let us say the owner has emigrated to America and leases the shabby little shop on the stand to a dry-cleaning depot or shoe-mender. Meanwhile the owner's agent learns that Tutu's man has bought the rest of the block for an average of R3 000 per square metre or over R10 million for 3 500 m^2. He now asks R8 000 per square metre or R4 million for his little piece, without which the Church can't hope to put up its lovely new Cathedral. Do you think that would be fair, that a man who doesn't even live in South Africa could hold up the development of the city and the Church, by holding out for a ridiculous price?"

"That doesn't sound right, Chaka," said Kazamulu, "but isn't that an isolated example?"

"Not at all, Kazamulu. Whenever the economy enjoys a spurt of growth land prices go up — especially in places which are needed for new developments. Usually they get to a point where the new developers fail because they pay too much for the land, or the buildings have to be of poorer quality. Then other developers see they can't afford to buy the land and cancel their plans and the economy slows down. Or else they may be forced to buy land further away from the city in a less suitable place. This is why you get leapfrogging of new townships with empty land between them and the other houses. This urban sprawl adds enormously to the cost of providing facilities as well as transport. Meanwhile, the landowners in the middle just sit and watch the value of their land go up — thanks to all the development around them to which they have contributed nothing."

"So what's the difference between this and a free market in land?" asked Alfred.

"Well, my brother," said Chaka, "taken together, owners of land ripe for development or re-development have a kind of monopoly position as against those who need to use the land. What's more, they haven't even created or added value to the ground they're selling, whereas other monopolists, such as S.A. Breweries, at least have to brew the stuff. Many goods and services have a limited shelf life or their producers have laid out money for raw materials and labour which they need to recover, and are therefore under some pressure to sell. This is not so with land. Land that has become ripe for new uses can very often still be used for grazing or parking or anything that does not require it to be developed properly, and the income will be enough to cover the owner's carrying costs, if any. Meanwhile, the owner bides his time waiting for the inevitable buyout at many times the price he paid for it. For to develop, the community needs land — it has no choice. That is why land ownership which is not subject to collection of rent becomes a kind of monopoly."

"And you reckon collecting natural rent will put an end to this nonsense?"

"Yes, and it will free up the market in land because people won't be able to afford to hoard land they don't use properly," said Chaka.

"Mdala, goodbye, and may the Lord truly bless you," said Kazamulu, standing up suddenly.

"What's the hurry? Where are you going, my brother?" asked Alfred.

"To seek an audience with His Grace the Archbishop!"

"What for, Kazamulu?"

"I want to show him how to get another Nobel Prize — only this time it will be for freeing the economy!"

12 CALL TO THE WEST

Year after year they voted cent, per cent.,
Blood, sweat, and tear-wrung millions –
            Why? for rent!
They roar'd, they dined, they drank, they swore they meant
To die for England – why then live? – for rent!
The peace has made one general malcontent
Of these high market patriots; war was rent!
Their love of country, millions all misspent,
How reconcile? by reconciling rent!
And will they not repay the treasures lent?
No: down with everything, and up with rent!
Their good, ill, health, wealth, joy or discontent,
Being, end, aim religion – rent, rent, rent!

Lord Byron

Just as Alfred thought, Chaka's talks were arousing great interest and it was not long before Petrus called again at Chaka's home, together with Dr Phalane and some of the others who had visited him in June.

"Yes, old man! I see you're still talking to all who care to listen, so I thought you wouldn't mind if we called again. We've had some visitors from America and they don't think much of these ideas," said Dr Phalane.

"I know you're right. But does it matter? The trouble is, we're so used to every new thing and idea, be it computers, capitalism, communism or women's lib, coming to us only after first being tried out overseas. But now we're beginning to realise that we in Africa are going to have to be the first to put into practice fresh principles in the art of government and economy, if we are to survive," said Chaka.

"In any event, I hope your American friends will forgive me if I turn the tables on them and offer *them* some advice for a change. I have some thoughts about how the West could benefit from introducing the changes I have been proposing for South Africa.

"After all, Henry George was himself American, and he came to his ideas about natural rent because of what he saw happening in his own country. Specifically, he was troubled by a curious paradox: The American West was being opened up and it was a period of great progress, growth and increasing prosperity, and yet at the same time poverty was also increasing. He puzzled over why this should be so.

"Then one day, while riding out in the country above San Francisco Bay, he saw in a flash of inspiration that this poverty was the inevitable result of the fact that rent, arising naturally from the growth of America, was not being collected for the benefit of America. You see, what had occurred over centuries in Europe took place within George's lifetime in America. So George, who was a brilliant observer, devoted his life to recording and interpreting information on the economic development in his country. He saw, and described in magnificent detail, the immense wealth which went to those who owned the land on which the nineteenth-century railroads and cities were built. He saw the taking, by a few, of the natural rent arising from the work of millions in opening up the mightiest economy ever known to Man.

"Why was he not heeded? Surely not just because he was rude to the economists when he spoke to them in the 1880s at Stanford, California? Was it because even the immigrant Americans, who arrived when land was no longer freely available and who had to work for others, were nevertheless enjoying a rapidly rising standard of living as well as opportunities and civil liberties they had never experienced before? Maybe they and their children after them shared the Great American Dream of becoming millionaires — in the days when it meant something!

"But for several decades now, it has been apparent that the break-neck pace of growth of the opening up of America is slowing down more and more, and that the divisions between rich and poor are widening, just as Henry George predicted they would. Despite Americans' can-do optimism, despite President Johnson's Great Society, a Health and Welfare budget of hundreds of billions of dollars, and Reaganomics, poverty is not going away. In 1984 the Census Bureau classified 34 million or 14,4% of Americans as poor. Over a third of blacks have incomes below the official poverty line. Of families headed by a woman, one in three is poor. As *The Economist* put it: 'If... time is allowed to slide by, the richest country in the world will enter the twenty-first century crippled by an unproductive and embittered underclass.'

"So the time is ripe for Americans to consider some of the questions they just brushed aside in the pell-mell growth eras. For example, why are they so unconcerned about the fact that 40% of the surface area of the U.S. belongs to government? Is this really the fabled home of individualism? Perhaps, without being aware of it, Americans fear they will lose out on those lands if they go private without collection of natural rent. Does this public ownership of land mean it is put to good use? How much of it lies idle — or is let at below market rentals?

"Another thing — I wonder how many Americans know that some 40% of all privately owned land is owned by 1% of the landowners?[2] Or that 3% is owned by 78% of the owners? Have they thought through the implications of the unimproved ground rents on those sites going to those individuals instead of direct to their Uncle Sam? Let us say for a moment that site user charges were adopted instead of taxation, and that as a result the pattern of land ownership changed to 40% of all private land owned by 20% of the owners. Wouldn't this have an enormous effect on productivity — bearing in mind that all economic activity on marginal sites would take place scot-free? It would mean in effect that America had rediscovered a prime under-used resource — its own land. Imagine the incentive to more efficient use of land this would provide. Both private owners and government would either release, or use productively, their under-used land holdings, rather than pay out site user charges for no income. All of a sudden land would become much more freely available and at the same time taxation could be, not merely reduced, but abolished! Add all this up and America could be where she was 100 years ago, with boundless new resources to tap and room to grow.

"With land freely available at the margin, and production there not only tax-free but rent-free, America's underclass would get out of the ghetto and into business. And if Reagan's tax cuts proved that business really responds to lower taxes, imagine how much more spectacular the response of business would be to the effective abolition of taxes on production of the marginal sites comprising, shall we say at a guess, 15% of the privately owned surface area of the U.S. With welfare funded from natural rent, just think about the effect that abolition of all company payroll deductions would have! When every \$1 of pay that the U.S. worker takes home costs his employer just that and no more, what effect would that have on job prospects for the poor? A well-known American economist called Arthur Laffer produced a graph with a curve like an upside-down saucer showing that as tax rates increase, Government revenues first go up, then level off, then go down. This so-called supply argument was used by Reagan to cut taxes and this led to a big recovery in the U.S. economy. The trouble with Laffer's curve is that lower taxes and economic growth alone do not eliminate the cause of poverty. Collecting natural rent instead of taxes does. Only then can the virtuous cycle of rising wealth leading at the same time to rising state revenues and reducing state welfare spending begin. Adding all this up, wouldn't you say that the U.S. has got this far with one hand tied behind its back and the other shooting itself in the foot?"

"Well, Chaka," said Doctor Phalane, "I would like to have heard what my American friends would say to all that. But would these ideas help the poorer countries of America?"

"Of course. Take Guatemala, for instance, where 2% of the population owns 70% of the land,"[2] said Chaka. "In El Salvador 50 families own over 70% of the land; 90% of farms are smaller than 10 hectares and occupy 25% of available farmland. Other Latin American figures are included in a table in this magazine, *Land and Liberty*, which Wilson Radebe brought me from the office the other day. It shows how, in most cases, the top 10% of the population own nearly half or more of all the land. The poorest 10% own, on average, only a little more than 1% of all the land."

LAND OWNERSHIP[3]
Percentage of total land area owned

	Top 10%	Bottom 10%
Barbados	95	0,5
Peru	93	0,1
Colombia	80	0,2
Mauritius	80	1,8
El Salvador	78	0,4
Guatemala	76	0,5
Jamaica	74	1,6
Nicaragua	67	0,1
Dominican Republic	63	2,0
Lebanon	57	1,0
Tunisia	53	0,5
Turkey	53	0,9
Morocco	49	1,0
Indonesia	48	3,0
Pakistan	46	0,4
Brazil	45	1,5
Panama	45	1,0
Mexico	37	0,3
Bangladesh	34	1,0
South Korea	28	2,0
Greece	27	2,6
Lesotho	22	3,0

After showing them the table Chaka continued, "If these spreads of land ownership are really the most efficient way to divide land in these countries, then site user charges won't disturb it. It's more likely, however, that they simply flow from non-collection of rent. So enormous gains in efficiency and productivity are possible once the process begins and land ownership becomes more widely spread.

"If the spread of land holdings elsewhere in Central and South America shows similar imbalances, then site user charges are surely the key to the survival of the current trend towards greater democracy. For if all the new governments do is carry out large-scale land expropriation, or condone squatter takeovers, this would simply lead to non-collection of rent from a somewhat larger number of owners — and the end result would be the return of military dictators.

"Mexico, for example, would no doubt benefit from privatisation of the *ejido*, the communal landholdings that cover half the arable land in the country. The land allotments could be valued so as to determine the initial rentals payable, and they could then be distributed free, subject to the new owners paying for the improvements on easy terms. This could provide the kind of boost to the Mexican economy that Taiwan and Japan achieved with their land reforms. Needless to say, if these principles were then applied to the rest of the country the benefit would be even greater."

"But Chaka, you've left out Brazil, which destroys your argument completely. Brazil has a land tax which is actually causing the forests of the Amazon jungle to be cut down at such a rate that scientists believe the ecology of the whole world will be fatally damaged," said Petrus.

"Good heavens, Petrus!" said Chaka. "Now I really am in trouble! So you've not only thought about what we've been saying, but done some research to see if it works."

"Oh! it was just that Wilson happened to tell me about it," said Petrus, looking a little sheepish at all this praise. "Anyway, in Brazil land tax is payable on unimproved land, which includes forests, so the landowners cut the forests down for ranching because the tax is reduced by 90% on land used for crops and pasture."

"That's very interesting, Petrus," said Chaka. "In fact, Wilson and I also discussed Brazil the other day. Apparently farmers there pay little or no tax, so businessmen buy land, which is a good investment with Brazil's 500% — 1 000% rate of inflation, show their business income as farming income and end up paying no tax. The government also gives tax credits for investments in certain schemes in the Amazon Basin. Since it is mainly the rich who benefit from tax credits, it means that all other taxpayers in Brazil are subsidising the rich to destroy the forests and the world's ecology."

"Well, then, that's just what I was saying," said Petrus triumphantly. "Land tax is a lot of hogwash and helps the rich!"

Petrus' friends were already beginning to laugh in anticipation of that comic look of terror covering Chaka's face again when the old man said calmly, "Well, not exactly, Petrus, because I haven't told you the craziest thing of all."

"What's that, mdala?" they cried.

"The land on which the forests stand is poor and no good for farming. There is plenty of good farmland elsewhere in Brazil. It is only the tax laws which make it worthwhile for businessmen to ranch there, even if the ranch itself runs at a loss — which it usually does.

"Now, if there were no taxes in Brazil and the government collected natural rent, the rate payable on land covered by forests would not necessarily change just because the trees were cut down. Moreover, there would be no question of an owner's losses on one piece of ground being offset against the site user charge payable on other property of his. Each piece of land would have its own rate according to its own value. No, there's no doubt about it, Petrus, that Brazilian story is just one of the many lunatic distortions caused all over the world by taxation. And the land tax they have there is nonsense, because it changes when the land is used for different purposes instead of simply being based on value. And furthermore, it is just one tiny tax in a jungle of other taxes. In fact, it's the tax jungle they should be doing away with, not the Amazon jungle," said Chaka, smiling.

"But Chaka, wouldn't your site user charge encourage some owners to develop land which for historical, cultural or ecological reasons should be left as it is?" asked Doctor Phalane.

"That is quite so, Doctor, but one of the other fundamental and natural duties of the State, in addition to collecting natural rent, is to ensure that all landowners observe their natural duty in regard to their land, which is to keep it in good condition — and that obviously includes the ecology, and the preservation of historical buildings. To give you an example, let us suppose that ranching on former Brazilian forest land is commercially profitable. Well then, that is one area where the Government would be naturally obliged to forbid a commercially profitable activity. Now when the Government does take steps to forbid commercially profitable, but ecologically harmful, activities the land value automatically takes this into account so the rate payable by the owner comes down accordingly. In the same way, historical buildings could be preserved by zoning their sites in a way that would prevent new development on them."

"Okay, you've convinced me. But what about Europe, Chaka? How would your system work there?" asked Petrus.

"Petrus, it was in the United Kingdom in the late nineteenth century that the ideas of Henry George aroused the most interest and received their greatest acclaim. His addresses in many centres, especially in Scotland and Ireland, drew large crowds and were a major factor in making the Land Question a major issue in British politics for several decades. As I told you a few weeks ago, Winston Churchill, then one of the Liberal Party's up-and-coming leaders, expounded George's ideas with his customary eloquence.

"Despite the fact that those debates have been long-since forgotten, the need for collection of rent has become more, not less, obvious. Decades of socialist redistribution, and some Tory success in bringing inflation down in the

Eighties, have done nothing to eliminate the root cause of poverty and unemployment.

"As in the U.S., land distribution in England is way out of kilter: 52% of the land is owned by just 1% of the population.[4] In Scotland 90% of the total area belongs to 1 500 landowners, while the remaining 10% is divided among the five million other inhabitants.[5]

"The effect of taxation on production at the margin, that is, poor areas with little or no taxable capacity, is perhaps more easily visible in the U.K. than elsewhere. The result has been that country areas in Scotland, Wales and the South-West, as well as once-important ports like Liverpool, have stood still or gone backwards while the areas around London in South-East England and a few other centres have surged ahead.

"Another interesting aspect is that by entering the European Economic Community, most of the United Kingdom has become an outlying area of this common market. At the same time, U.K. entry has strengthened the centre of gravity of the community based on the Rotterdam-Ruhr-Rhineland axis. Other areas on the perimeter are Portugal, the South of Italy and Greece.

"Now, if raising revenue from rent rather than taxes on production is better for a country, the same applies to an economic entity such as the E.C. This underscores perhaps more forcefully why Mrs Thatcher was right in objecting to the U.K. contributing more to the E.C. budget than it received. Clearly the U.K. and other outlying members of the E.C. should be net beneficiaries of its budget. This would not be charity. It would be the natural result of the benefits to the central areas, of the broadening of their markets, which would be reflected in their site values.

"Of course, the famous Square Mile in the City of London would still have astronomically high site values, reflecting the fact that it is still one of the three biggest financial markets in the world. This is despite technology, which, on the face of it, would appear to help trade in these markets by people who are not located in the financial centres themselves.

"Petrus, do you remember what I said that first night when you called me to see you and Vusi and the others? I said that what we were calling for was like the plea of Tolstoy to his fellow Russians before their Revolution. I also spoke of the Physiocrats, who pleaded with Louis XVI and their fellow aristocrats before the French Revolution of 1789 to impose the 'impôt unique' or single tax on the 'produit net' or net product of agriculture. This was to replace the maze of heavy and complicated taxes which burdened trade, transport and industry as well as the peasants. It is interesting to note that the idea of 'produit net' has become fashionable again in recent decades, as the tax man pays more attention to the value added or net product of a business enterprise than to the total sales or profits. And the Physiocrats' suggestion that the impôt be placed on agriculture alone wasn't as strange as we might think nowadays. At the time,

101

agriculture was by far the most important activity in the economy. In any event, once applied, it could easily have been extended to commerce and industry later. Who knows, if the aristocrats had heeded the Physiocrats, they might have saved themselves, spared France and Europe many upheavals, and set France far along the road to peaceful reform.

"But it's not too late even now for France to take a lead. As I have already told you, one of the few academics in the world to look seriously at the best way of collecting natural rent was the Frenchman V. Precy, whose proposals in 1930 included tenders to establish site rentals.

"Now, Petrus, as for the rest of your question, since our communications with the outside world have traditionally been via the Anglo-Saxon countries, it would be futile to pretend that we South Africans can say much about the rest of Western Europe. Yet there is little doubt that natural law works with equal force there. I spoke to you and the Doctor about the successful Danish experiment with land tax in 1960. Maybe one day research will throw new light on the role that German land enclosures, without collection of rent, played in bringing about the pressures that led to two World Wars.

"Getting back to the E.C., it could use a top-down approach to apply these principles. In other words, member states could work out their total land values on a macro-economic basis using agreed samples and methods. These could then be used as the basis for assessing E.C. budget contributions instead of government budgets as at present. This could be done fairly quickly. Afterwards the E.C. Commission or individual member states could look at ways to determine site rentals at the national level.

"By contrast, in other countries where site-value rating is widely used at local government level, as in South Africa and Australia, a bottom-up approach might be preferable.

"In any event, the application of these principles would undoubtedly release the enormous potential of the peoples of Western Europe. United action on a basis of common principle and practice would be a major step toward restoring the ancient unity of this continent. So once more it could be self-reliant in its defence, and a major force for peace and progress in the world."

13 CALL TO THE EAST

Marxists of the world unite. You, like us, have nothing to lose but the chains of a useless ideology.

Chaka Dlamini

"It's my turn now, Chaka," said Doctor Phalane. "You say your ideas are good not only for Africa but also for America and Western Europe. Does all this good news, in your opinion, also hold good for the East?"

"Well, Doctor," said Chaka, "let's look at Japan first. What can we say about a country which has shown such astounding progress and which even now shows no sign of having reached the pinnacle of its success? You will remember I spoke briefly about the Meiji Restoration of 1868, a key element of which was land reform and land tax. Obviously other factors, such as the commitment to universal education and the extraordinarily rich cultural heritage of Japan, played their part.

"Then again, we saw that less than a century later, in 1945, General Douglas MacArthur was worried because the land reform had degenerated to the stage where the smaller landlords were living in the towns taking up to two-thirds of the crops from their tenants. One feels that those high rents which MacArthur temporarily cut down, are back in place and that they have something to do with the present large number of absentee landlords. Perhaps site user charges would result in more owner-operated farms with a greater incentive to efficiency. Agriculture is not, at present, at the forefront of Japan's drive for efficiency. The 8,8% of the Japanese workforce employed on the land does not produce enough rice to meet domestic demand despite the fact that the Japanese consumer pays eight times the world price!

"In those mountainous islands only 15% of the land can be cultivated, and industrial, commercial and residential land values are amongst the world's highest. A two-bedroomed apartment in a centrally situated Tokyo building sold recently for $6,25 million! In 1988, prime commercial property in Tokyo was changing hands at $20 000 a square foot.[1] Given the small size and flimsy construction of these houses, land accounts for a higher proportion of bond payments than in any other leading nation. This may explain why Japan, until recently, despite massive trade surpluses, had such a low propensity to consume. In effect, much of these surpluses are rent, which ends up in a small number of institutional and other hands. Site user charges would change the picture by lowering the exorbitant cost of land and easing the access of individuals to residential land and of smaller business units to land for production.

"What's more, with the world wondering where the next Locomotive of demand is going to come from now that the American consumer spree is over, the recent unleashing of Japanese consumer power, if it were combined with incentives to produce even more efficiently, would provide a very handy impetus to the next cycle of growth in the world economy. It would also help put right the massive imbalance in world trade which threatens to upset the world financial system. Unfortunately, the Japanese Government is thinking of lowering income tax and increasing sales tax instead. This may put the long rule of the Liberal Democratic Party in real danger because the ordinary people will see it as letting off the rich and hitting them harder, while at the same time they still suffer from the high prices of land. In a nutshell, Doctor, a switch to site user charges would solve not only these problems of Japan's but also those of world trade.

"As regards Taiwan, I've already told you about its land reform programme, which formed the basis for its success, thanks to the application of some of these principles via Sun Yat-Sen. Some of these ideas have been adapted to good effect at local government level to promote urban renewal.[2] But if Taiwan is to maintain its momentum and avoid the distortions of uncollected rent, it would do well to return to its intellectual roots for renewed inspiration.

"Unlike Japan, the Philippine islands are rich in resources, good soil and climate, minerals, rivers and lakes. Yet 76% of the people live below the poverty threshold. Three-quarters of the people work on the land but only 25% own their own farms. The situation now is a little like that of Taiwan before its reforms. The Philippines' previous ruler, Marcos, claimed to be basing his abortive land reforms[3] on Taiwan's, and the World Bank advised him to introduce a land tax. *The Economist*, in this issue Wilson brought for me to read, sums up the course of action for the present leader Mrs Cory Aquino:

"*They* (that is, explained Chaka, Chiang Kai-Shek's followers) *have taken the 'offshore province' from abject poverty – in the early days, Taiwan was poorer than the mainland and its people stayed alive on a diet fit for sparrows – to the brink of a consumer boom. They did so by remoulding the structure of the economy: in 1952 agriculture's share of*

gross domestic product was 32% and industry's share was 22%; today, agriculture accounts
for less than 6% of GDP and industrial output for around half.

"The key was a 'land-to-the-tiller' programme of land reform first advocated by... Dr Sun Yat-sen, as a way of breaking up the land baronies of the mainland. When Chiang Kai-shek, a generation after Dr Sun's death, arrived in Taiwan, two-fifths of farmers did not own the land they tilled; had no security of tenure; and had to pay more than 50% of their harvest as rent. Much the same could be said of the Philippines, where land reform remains stuck in a mire of corruption and political cronyism."

Dr Phalane interrupted with a chuckle, "They call that boetie-boetie here."

Chaka grinned and continued: "The difference in Taiwan was that the reformers came from outside and had military power to back their social and economic planning.

"The first step, Mrs Aquino please note, was to extend lease tenure to a minimum of six years and to reduce farm rentals to a maximum of 37,5% of the average crop yield of the previous three years. The effect was a psychologically encouraging and immediate boost to tenant incomes. The second step, in 1951, was the sale of public land in easy instalments to 156 000 tenant families at a price fixed at 2,5 times the annual crop price. The final stage was a limit to individual land holdings – with dispossessed landlords reimbursed with government bonds and stocks. The result has been dramatic. Only 6% of farming families in Taiwan now work land they do not own either fully or in part.

"But the impact goes well beyond redressing rural inequalities. The dispossessed landlords no longer had an interest in local politicking; instead, they had an incentive, by selling or using as security for loans, the Government I.O.U.'s given them as compensation for their land, to enter – and so expand – the urban and industrial economies. Yesterday's landowner became today's small businessman, and is now becoming tomorrow's high-technology industrialist.

"Need we say more!" said Chaka. "Mrs Aquino, like us, needs to act decisively to avert revolution.

"Then there's the other great success story of the Far East, Hong Kong, where the free market free-for-all, low taxation and Chinese entrepreneurship have combined to create a powerhouse of production. Perhaps I'm spoiling the fun a bit if I point out that, with the Colony not collecting the full site value rental, amongst the biggest beneficiaries are the owners of Hong Kong's high-priced real estate. One wonders also what Lord Shaftesbury, who told the world about the terrible conditions under which British women and children worked in the factories and mines in the Industrial Revolution, would have to say about the working conditions in Hong Kong. Here in these cramped apartments families live and work around the clock assembling the millions of electronic gadgets that pour out of the island! Still, when the alternative is deportation to the Mainland who's going to complain? Nevertheless, the thought does occur that it might be in the Colony's long-term interest to collect that rent and plough it into education so that Hong Kong can maintain its lead when it returns to China in 1997.

"But let's look at one of the poorest Asian countries, Bangladesh. There the poorest 60% of households own only 9% of the land. Over half the population are landless or marginal peasants with not enough to live on, and in 1981-2, 40% of the workforce was unemployed. If site user charges were introduced in Bangladesh and India, who knows? The untouchables might just become the unbeatables as farmers on their own lands!"

"That's fine, Chaka, but I am sure that by the East Dr Phalane meant our socialist brothers in Russia and China," said Petrus.

"Okay," said Chaka, "though I don't know how many socialist brothers you'd find in either country these days! The failure of Marxism to deliver the goods has left both Russia and China groping their way away from socialist economics in much the same way that our Government first started retreating from apartheid — unwillingly, and all the time denying that basic principles would have to be changed!

"One of the many problems faced by China and the USSR, in their attempts at reform, is the absence of free markets to serve as a guide in the allocation of resources, including land and property. But allowing officials to determine land values would make things even worse. It should not be impossible for markets to develop, even if they begin only with state-owned enterprises trading with each other, because market activity would then increase as these enterprises dispose of outdated and uneconomic operations and new industries are started.

"The Russians and other East Europeans have a golden opportunity to apply the principles we have been discussing, simply by allowing individuals or companies to have land subject to a market-related annual user charge established by the auction system we have proposed for South Africa.

"The Chinese Communists are now in the process of returning some land to private ownership in order to boost agricultural production. It's ironic that in doing so, they are about to resurrect the evils of landlordism, which their erstwhile foes, the Nationalists under Chiang Kai-Shek, would never have done! For in privatising agriculture, Deng reportedly acknowledged this as the price that must be paid for efficiency and the incentive to produce. Nothing wrong with privatisation at all, Mr Chairman. But please forget about tax and remember rent!

"Not to be outdone, the USSR under Gorbachev has decided to let the Soviet farmer be master on the land by giving leases for 50 years or even longer, which can be passed down from father to son. Before we applaud them for being on the right track, however, we must ask some questions. Will the farmers be free to produce what they think the market wants, or will the government still tell them what to grow? What happens at the end of the lease to the improvements the farmers have made to their land — the dams, roads and buildings? Will the State just take them back, or will the farmers be free to sell them to the highest bidder? If the State takes them, what incentive will this reform give the farmer to improve the land? The Soviet Minister of Agriculture has said that the USSR will have a free-market system of agriculture only once there is an abundance of food. Given the past performance of the Soviet system of controls, this means never!

"The timid economic reforms introduced by perestroika are not nearly enough. Shortages of most consumer goods and food grow worse by the day, and the people are angry. Unless Gorbachev privatises state industries, perhaps by letting the workers have shares, and collects site-user charges, he has very little chance of breathing new life into the Soviet economy."

"And what about Eastern Europe, Chaka?" said Dr Phalane. "After the first fine flush of freedom from Russia they seem no better off."

"True," said Chaka. "Though in one respect they are much better off than Russia in that they have thrown out the ideology of Marxism. That, of course, does not mean they are all of a sudden eager to become capitalists. But it does mean they are in an excellent position to let free enterprise flourish. User charges on natural resources are still the key to success, even though they will be low initially because of the devastated state of their economies. This is the chance for Western bankers to make up for the folly of their misplaced lending to Third World countries in the seventies and early eighties. Provided the credit they extend to Eastern Europe is pinpointed for businesslike operations, there is every reason to believe they can be as successful in putting the Eastern European nations on their feet as the Marshall Plan was in resurrecting Western Europe after the Second World War."

"Now, Chaka, you're saying that socialism is a useless system," said Doctor Phalane. "I thought you said you weren't interested in politics."

"Doctor, it's the *economic* consequences of socialism that interest me," replied Chaka. "Socialism was an attempt — a clumsy and misguided attempt, as it turned out — to end the poverty caused by not collecting the rent. It failed because it taxed labour and capital instead of collecting that rent.

"I have always said that it is a natural duty of the State to care for those who are genuinely incapable of looking after themselves. Socialism promised to do this, and this is why many governments tried it. But in fact, so long as governments fail to collect natural rent, so long will they have to help the poor with massive welfare handouts. Secondly, socialist governments went one giant step further and tried to control and direct their economies. This meant they had to try to take the place of the free market mechanism in allocating resources and also that they got saddled with the job of running a wide variety of businesses. You know, Doctor, in some ways we in South Africa are very lucky."

"You must be crazy, old man," said Petrus.

107

"Well, it's like this, my friends! Apartheid has been tried in this country and been proved to be both unjust and an economic disaster. And in half the rest of the world, socialism has been given more than a fair trial and found to be the same. Now, Petrus, tell me. Wouldn't we be crazy to go and repeat the mistakes of socialism when we have so many proven examples of its failure? Do you agree that it would be just as stupid as wanting to start with apartheid all over again?"

"I'm not so sure, Chaka," said Petrus, although by now it seemed he lacked conviction.

"Well *I'm* sure. So now I'm going to let the facts about land reform speak to you instead. In another issue of *Land and Liberty*[4] there was a review of a book titled *The Peasant Betrayed – Agriculture and Land Reform in the Third World*. The authors, Powelson and Stock, studied 26 countries over a period of 20 years and they found that only where land reform was negotiated from peasant strength did the peasants make lasting gains. In most other cases, land was taken from the big land barons by the State, but whether the land was given to individual farmers or to government co-operatives, the peasants were no better off. This was because the governments controlled prices and in many other ways tried to order the lives of the peasants. Moreover, governments favoured city dwellers by paying low prices for farm produce and charging monopoly prices for fertilisers, seed and other inputs.

"In Tanzania, for example, different tribal customs and traditions were ignored or destroyed. Many people were forcibly removed by government edict and farms were often burned to stop the peasants from going back. The authors found that an economy is much more complicated than the imagination of any government, and that all peasant societies have their own ways of handling credit, supply, markets, savings, investments and spreading technological know-how. The State often abolishes these institutions instead of supporting them, thereby disrupting village life. As in Tanzania, the result of replacing the vision of the peasant with that of the State was a ruined economy.

"In Nicaragua the Sandinista government did not institute 'Land to the Tiller' reforms as in Taiwan but stuck to state co-operatives instead. Although the tenant farmers freely elected their co-operative committees, only government made the basic decisions.

"Only Taiwan, which we have already talked about, and South Korea were successful.

"In South Korea the large landowners had collaborated with the Japanese in the Second World War and the post-war government needed the peasant vote. So it did not interfere, and allowed prices to rise, merely helping consumers with subsidies where necessary. Instead of just growing rice, South Korean farmers began to produce other crops and livestock, and by 1964 one half of the land had been redistributed to two-thirds of the people on the land.

"The authors concluded that all the other governments they studied were unhelpful to the peasants, none of whom had ever chosen a state farm except under pressure. Real power to the masses meant freedom for the peasants to structure their own societies and to choose for themselves whether they wanted State, private or co-operative farming. In all the countries where the peasants lacked economic freedom, it was noted they lacked the political clout to bring it about. By the way, neither the Right nor the Left, neither the US nor the USSR nor the UN, seemed at all interested in seeing peasants enjoy meaningful political power.

"So there it is, my friends. It is no good freeing the land for the people if you don't also free the people. This socialism won't do. If we free our people economically, they will find a way of doing things. Look at the taxis. We didn't need the Harvard Business School or the ANC to tell us what to do. It just happened naturally. That's what we say. Just collect natural rent and leave the people alone.

"We have seen socialism and it doesn't work. Our brothers in the ANC who were in Tanzania and Angola can tell us. Capitalism is better than socialism at promoting economic growth, but nowhere does it kill poverty. My friends, we don't want failed old overseas ideas. We want something better. We want free land for free men.

"Petrus, I have had a good life and I am not worried about what happens to me. But I want something better for you and the Doctor and your children. That is why I speak like this, not from the arrogance of age."

14 BROAD SUNLIT UPLANDS

Workers and capitalists of the world unite! You have nothing to lose but the chains of taxation on labour and capital!

Chaka Dlamini

At this stage there was a knock on the door and Vusi Tshuma, who had been released from detention a few days before, came in, accompanied by some of the youngsters who were present the night Chaka was called out of bed. Doctor Phalane signalled to them to be quiet, and Chaka continued.

"In the darkest days of World War Two, when the lights of freedom had been extinguished in Europe and elsewhere, one of the Free World's greatest champions inspired people the world over to fight and die to regain that freedom. Churchill gave them a vision of civilisation moving on to broad sunlit uplands of greater prosperity and enlightenment.

"You see, he knew that people *need* a vision. The Bible says, 'Where there is no vision the people shall perish.' (Proverbs 29:18). But what vision do the ANC, the UDF, or the PAC offer us? Freedom from apartheid, yes. And then what? A 'people's' government like that of the USSR or Mozambique? Or a democracy like that of the U.S. or U.K.? The way I see it, both of these are undesirable and difficult to achieve for us.

"Our problems would vanish like the morning mist were other countries to provide us with happy examples to follow. It would be good to think that the principles we have spoken of might serve as an inspiration for renewal of an America whose economy seems no longer able to deliver both the guns and the butter required for superpower status. Or that Japan could see these principles as the basis both for allowing its people to enjoy more of the fruits of their success and for assuming the responsibilities expected of such a wealthy nation. Or that the ruling cliques of Russia and China would at last heed their Tolstoys and Sun Yat-Sens and allow free men and free land to raise their nations to renewed

110

grandeur.

"Alas, the inertia of the systems in these and other countries we have discussed is such that they will probably only be tinkered with, not changed in any fundamental way.

"Only in South Africa do we know that the forces at play will most certainly end the established order. 'Reform or die,' said P.W. Botha. 'The people shall govern,' say the ANC. But those forces are so balanced that none of the players will succeed in imposing their ideologies on the others.

"We all know South Africa will change. But whether for better or worse, whether through negotiation or catastrophe, nobody knows. What we do know is that if that change is to be peaceful, new ideas will have to emerge.

"And if men see that the new ideas do not threaten them, then they may at last be freed from the tensions and fears that prevent hearts from opening to the need for us to find each other. Yes, there are vested interests in our country, as there are in other countries, which one might normally expect to reject new ideas. But these are not normal times, and those groups now have a greater vested interest in supporting those new ideas which alone can prevent all that we have built up here from being swept into the oblivion of chaos and destruction.

"I hope, indeed I believe, nay I know, that somehow, somewhere, some of the ideas that have been given to us, that we have spoken of together, will be useful in helping us find our way through. And they may give birth to other ideas that we must yet discover. I pray therefore that Divine Providence will guide us so that the words of the old Roman may be proved true: *Ex Africa aliquid semper novis*, or 'Out of Africa always something new'. In this case, let it be a beacon of light, a way of hope for ourselves and for all men, from what was once called the Dark Continent.

"Now, my children, the French had their Turgot, the Americans their Henry George, the Russians Tolstoy and the Chinese Sun Yat-Sen and you have only old Chaka here. So it may be difficult for you. But then again, these ideas are rooted in the very nature of man and the heart of Africa. That is why I think they will succeed. So, my friends, you asked me to speak and I have. I can say no more now. You must do what you will."

"Old man," said Vusi, "we have heard from our brothers about you these last few days and we believe what you say to be good and true. Not only may you continue to speak freely, but you must!"

Murmurs of assent and laughter filled the crowded room.

"From now on," continued Vusi, "it is not you that is on trial but all of us here. For the message you have given us is truly the way for Africa, not what we have heard from overseas, and it is now up to us to understand it. Hambe kahle baba."

111

CHAPTER NOTES

Chapter 2

1. *The Freedom Charter*, adopted at the Congress of the People, Kliptown, 26 June 1955. Reproduced as an advertisement by the UDF in The Star, 26 June 1987.

Chapter 3

1. Lord Soames, quoted in an article: *How Tax Prevents Prosperity* by Emile Woolf and John D.Allen, *Management Today* April 1987.

2. Commission of Enquiry into the Tax Structure of the Republic of South Africa, known as the Margo Commission, made its report in November 1986. Its main recommendation, the Comprehensive Business Tax, was rejected by the government. Value Added Tax (VAT), an alternative recommendation of the Commission, was later accepted as a replacement for General Sales Tax (GST).

3. SITE: Standard Income Tax on Employees. This is part of the Pay as You Earn (PAYE) system. The tax deducted from an employee's pay under SITE is final.

4. Richard Rose. *The Makings of a Do-it-yourself Tax Revolt. Public Opinion* August/September 1980.

Chapter 4

1. V. Precy. *La Rente Fonciere – son essence, sa loi, sa valeur sociale et financiere, et le moyen precis de l'evaluer.* Paris: Bureaux de la League pour la Reforme Fonciere. 1930. Quoted in an article by David Redfern, *Land & Liberty* May/June 1985.

Chapter 5

1. Victor Lebrun. *Leo Tolstoy and Henry George.* July 1966 issue of *Progress*, a magazine published by A E Hutchinson, 32 Allison Avenue, Glen Iris, S.E.6. Australia and reproduced by the Public Revenue Education Committee, 705 Olive St., Room 308, St. Louis, Mo. 63101 Chestnut 1-4350 (President Noah D. Alper).

2. Tholstrup, Knud. *Economic Liberalism.* 1 Vester Farings Gade, DK 1648, Copenhagen V, Denmark.

Chapter 12

1.   Land Ownership Survey by U.S. Department of Agriculture.

2.   *Incentive Taxation*, June 1983. 2000 Century Pl. (238), Columbia, MD. 21044. USA.

3.   U.S. Agency for International Development, quoted in George Thomas Kurion, *The New Book of World Rankings*, New York: *Facts on File Publications*, 1984 pp. 162-3. Reproduced in *Land and Liberty*, May 1987.

4.   *Land and Liberty*, January 1983.

5.   *Land and Liberty*, January 1988.

Chapter 13

1.   *The Economist* September 9, 1989 p 21.

2.   *Financial Mail*, Johannesburg. February 27, 1987. p 84.

3.   See *Land and Liberty*, March 1987 for reasons for its failure.

4.   *Land and Liberty*, January 1989. *"The Peasant Betrayed..."* was published by the Lincoln Institute of Land Policy, (1987), Oelgeschlager, Gunn & Hain.

BIBLIOGRAPHY

Bank, Ronald (Editor) *Costing the Earth* Shepheard-Walwyn in association with Centre for Incentive Taxation. London 1989.

Churchill, Winston. *The People's Rights* Jonathan Cape, London. Republished 1970.

Davenport & Hunt. *The Right to the Land* David Philip, Cape Town 1974.

de Kiewiet, C.W. *A History of South Africa – Social & Economic* Oxford University Press 1941. Reprinted 1978.

George, Henry. *Progress and Poverty* Robert Schalkenbach Foundation. N.Y. Reprinted 1974.

Harrison, Fred. *The Power in the Land* Shepheard-Walwyn, London 1982.

Letsoalo, Essy M. *Land Reform in South Africa – A Black Perspective* Skotaville Publishers, Johannesburg, 1987.

Li, Dr K.T. *Economic Transformation of Taiwan* Shepheard-Walwyn, London. 1988.

Louw, Leon & Frances Kendall. *South Africa – The Solution* Amagi Publications, Bisho, Ciskei 1986.

MacLaren, Leon. *The Nature of Society* Martlett Press, London

Smith, Adam. *The Wealth of Nations* Everyman's Library.